ROCKY RIVER, OHIO

THE REMARKABLE STORY OF A QUINTESSENTIAL AMERICAN SUBURB

Doug Kurkul

Copyright © 2025 by Doug Kurkul
Publisher: K Executive Group

ISBN 978-1629673141 (Paperback)
ISBN 978-1629673172 (Hardcover)

All rights reserved. No part of this book may be reproduced, transmitted, downloaded, reverse engineered, decompiled, or stored in any form or by any electronic, digital or mechanical means, including information storage and retrieval systems or artificial intelligence, without written permission from the author, except in the case of a reviewer, who may quote brief passages embodied in critical articles or in a review.

Trademarked names are used throughout this book. Rather than use a trademark symbol with every occurrence, names are used in an editorial fashion, with no intention of infringement of the respective owner's trademark.

The information in this book is distributed on an "as is" basis without warranty. Although every precaution has been taken in the preparation of this book, neither the author nor the publisher shall have any liability to any person or entity with respect o any loss or damage caused or alleged to be caused directly or indirectly by the information contained in this book.

Doug Kurkul, K Executive Group, 20235 North Cave Creek Rd, STE 104, PMB 302, Phoenix, AZ 85024

Cover Design: Tatiana Fernandez
Interior Formatting: Wise Media Group

v25-1016

ALSO AVAILABLE FROM THE AUTHOR

It's a Beautiful Day for Baseball: The National Pastime in the 1960s.

Portrait of a Franchise: An Intimate Look at Cleveland Indians Baseball During the Rockin' Sixties

Acknowledgements

The author is also indebted to those who have helped to document and preserve Rocky River history and advance its natural beauty through the decades, including and not limited to, Elizabeth Anderson, Phil Ardussi, Tom Barrett, Bill Barrow, Audra Bednarski, Carol Benyo, Melissa Bialko, Don Bierut, Pamela Bobst, Rita Bock, Betsy Gibson Burger, Patrick Burke, Kenneth Burney, Mary E. Case, Jim Chillemi, George A. "Sunny" and Marlys Christensen, Gay A. Christensen-Dean, City of Rocky River, David Cook, Jan Cipriani, Jack Clowser, John and Mary Corry, Susan Crane, Nicholas Cronin, Elizabeth Danielson, Laura Dean, Russell Dean, Edward Delzani, Jenny Dieringer, Ed Dowen, Dan Dugan, Harlow Eichler, Charles Emrick, Karla Ware Erb, Vic Erml, Jim and Sue Evans, Rev. Jon Fancher, Jenny Fisher, David Furry, Ron Gable, Jeanne Gallagher, Stacey Ganor, Richard Garrett, librarian Michael Garrison, Marge Gerard, Mrs. Earl Gibbs, William (Hoot) Gibson, Jean Gilbert, Harris Gillespie, Ginni Going, Sue Gragel, Nancy Gustafson, Ann Gynn, Don Harbaugh, David Harris, John Heffner, Betsey Heil, Gregory Helms, William Henson, David Hollis, Thomas J. Hunt, Harry Jacobs, Jill James, Ed and Marty Kennedy, Eleanor Kenney, Scott Kermode, Matt Knickman, Eve Arslanian Kurkul, Betsy Lanzen, Jeanette Lewis, John Lonsak, Suzanne Lydrickson, the MacBeth family, Catherine Manzo, Daniel Marsalek, Earl Martin, Richard Maturi, Cheryl McCoy, Heather McCrea, Sam McDowell, Sean McGettrick, Jean McQuillan, Maude Micheal (whose financial support permitted the purchase of the Brodbeck collection of Cowan pottery), Christina Morris, Alfred Morton, Sally Mylett, Jack Nickels, Mike O'Boyle, Russ and Phoebe Olson, Geof Pelaia, Ralph Pfingsten, Josephine Hoag Pleasance, Joseph Ptak, Harlan Radford, Peter J. Rea, Ruth Regula, Ralph Richards, Rocky River Chamber of Commerce, Rocky River Historical Society, Dr. Gordon and Lucy Rodeen, Jay Rounds, Bill and Bobbie Rudge, Nina Rushbar, Jim Sanders, Cynthia Schafer, George Scherma, Jim and Lynn Schieda, Sophia Schlather, James Seidel, Helen Sheppard, Paul Shipp, Dr. Michael Shoaf, Sandy Sill, Brian Sindelar, Byron Spooner, Dale Spooner, Sharon Spooner, Earl Stafford, Fred and Nancy Stover, Stacey Staub, S.F. Stein, Michael Thomas, Roberta Trutko, Don Umerley, George and Eleanore Von Hasse, Joyce Waltz-Umerley, John Weedon, Mabel Wenban, as well as librarians Katherine E. Wilder and Helen Williams.

Table of Contents

Acknowledgements 3

Image Index 7

Foreword 11

Preface 13

Today's Quintessential Suburb 15

A British Colonel's Infamous Landing 17

A Grand Vision 21

Becoming a Bustling Little Township 25

Reuben Wood's Presidential Near-Miss 29

Bridging the River 33

The First Churches 39

The Second Generation of Rocky River Businesses (1850 to 1900) 43

Impact of the Railroads 47

Pottery Shards a Century Later 53

A Country Club and a Yacht Club 55

Military Matters in Rocky River 67

Neighbors to the East: Lakewood 71

Clifton Beach's Life and Legacy 75

Daniel Eells, Lee Wilson and Sunset Point 81

A Civic Response to Drownings 85

The Van Dorn Family 87

A Brewing Magnate's Estate and Legacy 89

A Well-Connected Attorney 91

Streets with Recognized Names 93

Building Schools during the Baby Boom 99

The Greenhouse Capital of the Nation 105

The Third Wave of Memorable Businesses (1900 to 1950) 107
The Hotel Westlake's Storied History 115
The Mayor's Office 121
Neighbors to the West: Bay Village and Westlake 127
Rocky River Day 133
When Bowling Was Big 135
A Civic Response to Drug Abuse 137
The City's Shortest Street 139
The Day Pro Wrestling Didn't Come to River 141
The Fourth Generation of Rocky River Businesses (1950 to present) 143
Rerouting Downtown 161
Civic Improvements 163
Restoring the Clock Tower 165
Neighbors to the South: Fairview Park 167
Sports Figures Calling Rocky River Home 171
Sammy Kaye, Michael Stanley, the Arts and Media 175
The Emerald Necklace 183
Lakewood Park Cemetery 185
The Promising Future 189
About the Author 191
Appendix A: When Selected Rocky River Residential
Streets Were First Developed 193
Appendix B: Rocky River Chamber of Commerce Members (as of August 2025) 199
Appendix C: List of Greenhouses and Truck Gardens in 1927 203
Bibliography 205

Image Index

Figure 1 - Chief Pontiac (John Mix Stanley) 18

Figure 2 - Colonel John Bradstreet (by Thomas McIlworth 1764) 18

Figure 3 - Business tycoon Datus Kelley (public domain) 26

Figure 4 - The Silverthorn shown in a postcard (courtesy of Harlan Radford). 28

Figure 5 - Governor Reuben Wood (public domain)..29

Figure 6 - The 1910 bridge carried automobiles, streetcars and pedestrians. (Author's Collection) Published by Braun Postcard Co., Cleveland, Ohio 35

Figure 7 - 1980 Bridge Demolition and Construction (author's collection) 36

Figure 8 - Postcard showing the Hilliard Boulevard bridge (author's collection) 37

Figure 9 - Interior of 1847 Church building at 3300 Wooster Road (courtesy of Zillow) 39

Figure 10 - Courtesy of Rocky River Presbyterian Church...41

Figure 11 - An 1874 graphic advertisement for picnics and excursions at Tisdale (Sunset) Point. 45

Figure 12 - The Dummy Railroad was a short-lived passenger line as shown in this postcard (courtesy of Harlan Radford) 48

Figure 13 - The Norfolk & Western Train Station as seen in a 1970 postcard. (Courtesy of Harlan Radford) 49

Figure 14 - The Rocky River Train Station (watercolor painting by Marilyn Phyllis) (author's collection) 49

Figure 15 - Former streetcar station at 715 Wagar Road (courtesy of Google).........51

Figure 16 - Part of the Cowan Pottery collection at the Rocky River Public Library. 54

Figure 17 - (Graphic courtesy of Westwood Country Club)...56

Figure 18 - An earlier CYC clubhouse as depicted in a postcard. (Courtesy of Harlan Radford) 57

Figure 19 - Ice Jam on the Rocky River (author's collection) 59

Figure 20 - Ice Jam on the Rocky River (author's collection) 59

Figure 21 - The 1910 Winton Six 60

Figure 22 - Past Commodore Bill Rudge, left, with Joseph Kurkul on a CYC road trip in the early 2000s...61

Figure 23 - Mouse Island in Lake Erie 62

Figure 24 - Paintings of the Rocky River (author's collection) 63

Figure 25 - Home at 240 Cornwall Rd. once owned by banker W.S. Brown (courtesy of Zillow) 64

Figure 26 - The Edmund Fitzgerald freighter (courtesy of Greenmars CC BY-SA3.0)..............65

Figure 27 - Congressman Clifton B. Beach of Rocky River (public domain) 75

Figure 28 - Beach School (courtesy of Rocky River Public Schools) 77

Figure 29 - 21565 Aberdeen Road (courtesy of Zillow) 77

Figure 30 - House dating to 1890 was summer home to a founder of baseball's American League (author's collection) 78

Figure 31 - Sunset Point on the right during the Frank Mosier era. (Ken Winters, U.S. Army Corps of Engineers) 83

Figure 32 - Following the 1992 fire at 19420 Frazier Drive (author's collection).....................88

Figure 33 - House being completely rebuilt retaining only the historic facade (author's collection) 88

Figure 34 - Leonard Schlather Painting (RR Public Library) 90

Figure 35 - The Breitenstein House at 265 Cornwall (courtesy of Zillow) 92

Figure 36 - Century home at 1223 Allen Court dating to 1919 (courtesy of Zillow) 94

Figure 37 - The 141-year-old home at 539 Linda Street (author's collection) 95

Figure 38 - Matthew Groner's dog, Roxy, strikes a pose at the entrance to Wagar Beach. (Matthew Groner) 98

Figure 39 - 1970 Kensington Karnival promo photo (author's collection) 100

Figure 40 - The Primett Building, Rocky River's first brick structure (author's collection).....109

Figure 41 - Classic postcard showing downtown more than 100 years ago. (Courtesy of Harlan Radford) 110

Figure 42 - Candyland has brought joy to many hundreds of customers. (Permission of Bill Osgood and The Original Candyland) 112

Figure 43 - Postcard view of the back of the Hotel Westlake (author's collection) 115

Figure 44 - The Westlake being renovated in 1983. (author's collection) 119

Figure 45 - The Westlake on a beautiful recent spring day. (author's collection)....................119

Figure 46 - Mayor Schwenk's house as seen now at 852 Elmwood (courtesy of Zillow) 123

Figure 47 - The Knoble home at 18989 Schlather Lane (courtesy of Zillow) 125

Figure 48 - Huntington Water Tower (courtesy of Cleveland State Library Special Collections) 128

Figure 49 - Lawrence Mansion before it became a hospital (courtesy Bay Village Historical Society) 130

Figure 50 - The 1853 Crocker home in Westlake (courtesy of Zillow) 131

Figure 51 - Jeff Windahl of Roslyn Drive at 1971 Rocky River Day (author's collection).......133

Figure 52 - Otto's Brauhaus Restaurant as depicted in a postcard. 144

Figure 53 - Victoria Station restaurant company logo. 146

Figure 54 - Former Indians pitcher Steve Bailey with author Doug Kurkul at Bearden's Restaurant. 147

Figure 55 - Postcard depicting the Harbor View Motel. Photo by Harold Ingall (author's collection) 149

Figure 56 - American Legion Post 451, located off Linda Street. (author's collection) 150

Figure 57 - Herb's Tavern on a recent summer day. (author's collection)................................153

Figure 58 - The former Wooster Road office of Dr. Dean (author's collection)......................155

Figure 59 - One of the six Casey's Drive-In restaurants was on Center Ridge Road. 159

Figure 60 - Louise Gallagher painting of Rocky River Park courtesy of Rocky River Historical Society. Greeting cards available through the Historical Society. 164

Figure 61 - Rocky River Clock Tower as seen in 2025 (author's collection)............................165

Figure 62 - Second baseman Joe Gordon (courtesy of Cleveland Indians/Guardians)............172

Figure 63 - Entertainer Sammy Kaye (courtesy of Wikipedia)...176

Figure 64 - Michael Stanley induction into RRHS Hall of Fame. At right is Eve Kurkul, president of the RRHS Alumni and Parents Association. (author's collection).......................178

Figure 65 - The Michael Stanley Band in concert at Ashland University in 1982 (Photo: Shari Burley) 178

Figure 66 - Expired trademark for Mr. Jingeling. (public domain) 182

Figure 67 - Pitcher George Uhle (public domain) 186

Figure 68 - Pitcher Clint Brown (public domain) 186

Figure 69 - This postcard, mailed in 1959, shows four Rocky River scenes. (author's collection) 191

Figure 70 - Runners race down Beach Cliff Blvd. (author's collection) 194

Foreword

By
City Council President David Furry

Rocky River? It's a special place to grow up (although you might not know it at the time!), raise a family and locate a business.

Growing up in Tangletown, we had the endless game of wiffleball at Goldie's front yard, Haunted Houses at Corpus' house, Putt Putt golf at Connelly's, bike ramp jumping at Sparks's not to mention the annual block parties. You jokingly called it "The Bubble" but after you left Rocky River for other communities you realized that it is a great place to raise a family...and you move back.

I have lived in this city for nearly 50 years of my 60-plus years on this planet and have served on City Council for nearly 20 years, currently as President. I view myself as a placeholder for those that have served before me, looking out for both the interest of the City as well as the residents.

Rocky River is consistently in the top 5 suburbs as rated by *Cleveland* Magazine, #2 this past year and #1 the year prior. Plain and simple, it's a Great City on a Great Lake!

Read on to learn a great deal more about Rocky River.

David Furry, City Council President

Preface

It is often said that no matter where life takes us, we never forget where our life's journey began. I suspect that truer words are seldom spoken.

In the years since I graduated from Rocky River High School, I earned two college degrees, traveled in 36 countries and resided in six states plus Washington, D.C. I have worked in a variety of capacities, currently as CEO of the primary association serving the $50 billion metalcasting industry. I have been privileged to meet U.S. Presidents, cabinet members, a Supreme Court justice, lawmakers, Olympians, sports Hall of Famers, military commanders, extraordinary educators, and countless business leaders.

These many years later, I'm struck by the seminal role my hometown has played in my life, setting the stage for every experience that followed. I'm not alone. This community has a special place in the hearts of tens of thousands of people. Those who live – or have lived – here know first-hand of the tremendous quality of life and unique advantages it offers.

Rocky River has a remarkable story that I am excited to share. The formula for the City's successful evolution has been large doses of vision, dedication, hard work, perseverance, problem-solving, faith, free enterprise, unity, and, yes, good fortune. Throughout the journey, local leaders also emphasized education, arts, culture, recreation, plus transportation. That formula has allowed this special community to seize every opportunity and to address every challenge.

As you read on, you will see names that are part of the Rocky River story in ways small and large, names like Amelia Earhart, Datus Kelley, Arnold Palmer, Reuben Wood, Joe Gordon, Sammy Kaye, Philip Sheridan, Emily Macbeth, George Steinbrenner, Jess Bell, Red Gerard, Michael Stanley, Earl Martin, Pat McCormick, Rutherford Hayes, Sophia Schlather, Jimmy Doolittle, Lee Wilson, Jacob Silverthorn, Nev Chandler, James Petro, Sunny Christensen, Martin Savidge, Bob Hope, Daniel Eells, Yogi Berra, Nina Blackwood, William McKinley, Charles Lindbergh, Clifton Beach, Guy Cowan, and many others. Since life in Rocky River is closely integrated with that of the neighboring communities of Lakewood, Bay Village, Westlake and Fairview Park, chapters are devoted to those cities, as well.

The pages that follow are undoubtedly influenced by the author's own experience. Like so many others, I enjoyed the city parks, competed in Little League, fished at the pier and Bates Pond, enjoyed campouts at Elmwood Park, attended Sailing Camp at CYC, pretended to study at the public library while holding a girlfriend's hand, and received a great education from dedicated teachers. I learned about money by cutting lawns up and down Beach Cliff Boulevard and by working summer jobs at Bearden's (still going strong), the Silverthorn, and the City Service Department. My first stock trade at age 10 was shares of Lee Wilson Engineering, headquartered one block from our home, and my first public speech was presented at American Legion Post 451 less than a mile from home. Eve Arslanian Kurkul, my mother, served as President of six Rocky River civic organizations, and CYC named the Kurkuls the Family of the Year in 1990, all of which taught me the value of community service. Even the best day of my life – my 2002 wedding to my beloved bride Dr. Wen Kurkul – was in Rocky River.

It is my hope that every reader will learn some new things, have some pleasant memories rekindled, and be inspired by the story of vision and determination in this remarkable City's evolution into a quintessential American suburb.

Today's Quintessential Suburb

Residents know of Rocky River's attributes first-hand, but external accolades provide impartial confirmation. The suburb was recently named one of the nation's 100 safest cities. The public schools are among the best in Ohio – ranked number five out of 903 in the state, in fact, by *U.S. News* in August 2025. Rocky River perennially ranks number one or two in *Cleveland* magazine's best suburbs list. In 2025, the City was listed among the 15 finest suburbs in the entire state by *Niche* magazine.

In the most recent Census, Rocky River's population was 21,755, its highest mark in 50 years. Whereas most inner suburbs are losing residents, Rocky River is bucking that trend. The median family income is a comfortable $93,000 and the median home value is $327,000.

Longtime trusted realtors such as Kelley McNamara Meyer, James Umerley, Meredith Hardington and Kim Crane will point out that the community offers a wide range of quality housing options from luxurious single-family homes to modern townhomes to condos and apartments. Many homes have been modernized and enlarged. And it would be difficult to find any community where residents devote more love and care to maintaining beautiful lawns and landscaping, and decorating their homes for the holidays.

Nearly two-thirds of adult residents have completed at least one college degree which is another amazing characteristic. Through the years, Rocky River residents have included members of Congress, professional athletes, authors, artists, cartoonists, musicians, broadcasters, journalists, captains of American industry, physicians, attorneys and many other noteworthy individuals.

The City spans just 5.6 square miles, about 20 percent of which is water. Remarkably, the city offers access to at least nine different parks. The highly recognized school system consists of a high school, middle school, intermediate school, and an elementary school. The City is also home to a handful of non-public schools and nursery schools. Another civic treasure, the Rocky River Public Library, has 160,000 items in its collection and is home to the world-class Cowan Pottery Museum, displaying and retaining items made in Rocky River a century ago.

Providing sound stewardship is longtime Mayor Pamela Bobst, a highly dedicated City Council, law director, boards and commissions, as well as the City's workforce. One of this book's chapters includes information about each of the City's mayors and their achievements through the years. The Police Department helps make Rocky River one of the country's safest communities. The firefighters' proficiency was seen as recently as summer 2025 when they bravely battled a blaze at Rocky River Brewing in intense summer heat. Surveys show high levels of citizen satisfaction with local services. The Mayor and Council keep channels of communication open with the employees, their representatives, and the community.

Rocky River is blessed with a thriving business community. A family could eat out at a restaurant every Saturday night starting in January and still not exhaust all of the possibilities by year's end. Many dozens of locally owned businesses provide nearly every product and service imaginable. Meanwhile, nationally known brands such as Whole Foods Market, Ace Hardware, and Starbucks Coffee augment the quality of life. A list of all Chamber of Commerce members is printed in Appendix B.

Of course, the story begins with the tremendous advantages of the City's unique location. To the north is Lake Erie, one of the five Great Lakes, offering boating, water skiing, swimming and fishing. To the east is the Rocky River itself, a navigable river where three islands were combined into one to become the home of an outstanding yacht club. Also to the east is the Metropolitan Park valley, part of the Emerald Necklace that encircles Cleveland. Rounding out Rocky River's geographic advantages is the ease of getting to downtown Cleveland for live theater, concerts and major-league sports; to the international airport to the south; and to attractions such as Cedar Point to the west.

In the late 1800s, Rocky River's bucolic countryside and fresh air made it an attractive locale for weekend getaways and second homes for the wealthy who hoped to escape for a time from the rapidly industrializing Cleveland. From the dawn of the 20th Century, an area that originally was heavily forested with few signs of civilization (other than an Indian burial ground and a rough Indian path running east to west), gradually evolved into the greenhouse capital of the nation and then into a thriving suburb offering an outstanding quality of life. And so Rocky River evolved gracefully and steadily from part of Rockport Township in 1819, to a hamlet in 1893, a village in 1903 and a city in 1930.

Now, let's look back at some of the region's earliest recorded history and the story of a disgraced British military official.

A British Colonel's Infamous Landing

An impressive array of attractive public and private parks help make Rocky River a quintessential suburb. Each of these parks – located in neighborhoods throughout the community – offers different attractions, from sports fields to walking trails to sandy beaches to a fishing pier.

Bradstreet's Landing Park on the shore of Lake Erie – formerly known as Lake Edge Park – is visited by residents on a daily basis today but also has a fascinating history tracing back to those uncertain times following the conclusion of the French and Indian War (1754-1763).

Readers will recall that in the mid-1700s, several European powers were battling to control faraway territories, obsessed with the commercial and military advantages such dominance would bring. One of the most intense rivalries pitted the British and French, who engaged in hostilities not only in North America but also in the Caribbean, Europe and Asia. Here on this continent, France had the advantage of allied Indian warriors. Yet, Britain outlasted the French in a series of armed conflicts. The signing of the Treaty of Paris on February 10, 1763 signified a decisive British victory, a restructuring of global power, and the end of French claims to lands in North America.

Despite the military victory, Great Britain's North American headaches were expanding. Chief Pontiac and other influential Indians led a rebellion of unified Indian tribes (Chippewa, Ottawa, Potawatomi) against the British which simmered for a couple of years and then erupted full-scale in May 1763 at Fort Detroit.

Figure 1 - Chief Pontiac (John Mix Stanley)

Despite sustained attacks, the Indians were never able to capture the fort as they received diminished assistance from the French. After several Indian setbacks elsewhere along the Great Lakes, Chief Pontiac conceded defeat to Sir William Johnson. Pontiac and most of his followers retreated from Detroit to Ohio.

Great Britain turned its attention to continued exploration, trade, and repositioning of military and civilian personnel. One of the key figures was British Colonel John Bradstreet, who was born in 1714 and grew up in Nova Scotia. Military leadership was in his blood, as his father was also a British lieutenant, though he died when John was just seven years old. As an adult, John Bradstreet had led the successful British campaign over the French at Fort Frontenac in 1758, a key milestone in the French and Indian War.

Figure 2 - Colonel John Bradstreet (by Thomas McIlworth 1764)

A British Colonel's Infamous Landing

Fast forward to 1764 and Colonel Bradstreet was leading an armed transport of military men, teamsters, and some friendly Indians in dozens of boats that made several runs along the Great Lakes. It was in this context that in August 1764, Bradstreet led 2,300 men on dozens of seacraft from Fort Niagara to Fort Detroit, with stops along the way at the Cuyahoga River and the Rocky River on August 18 and August 19, 1764, respectively. They reached Fort Detroit without incident. Bradstreet's mission was to relieve troops on duty, take possession of prisoners, negotiate with Indians, and then depart before the onset of winter.

He initiated his return trip in October with 1,500 men, 59 boats, one barge and nine canoes. The group made a stopover in Sandusky, where a British outpost had been ravaged by Indian attacks. While there, he sought a treaty with local Indians who expressed no interest in smoking a peace pipe. Discouraged with his lack of progress, Bradstreet ordered his crew to hastily depart and sail east, with the intent of stopping that evening at the Rocky River harbor where the plan was to encamp safely on the northerly most island between the river's west and east channels (there were originally three islands that were combined to form the current Yacht Club island).

Darkness convinced Bradstreet to instead spend the night at today's Bradstreet's Landing Park. The date was October 18, 1764. His exhausted crew retired for the evening without removing provisions from boats, a massive mistake.

That night, a storm with surging waves sent numerous boats out to sea, permanently lost. Losing the boats would have been a tremendous blow under any circumstances but the disappearance of valuable armaments, provisions and baggage compounded the tragedy. It took three days in unseasonably cold and wet weather to make repairs to the remaining craft. Without enough boats, the men alternated on making the long trip to Fort Niagara via boat or on foot, crossing hills and rivers. At least one man was documented to have died on the return walk after having eaten poison hemlock.

The event came to be known as Bradstreet's Disaster, and British Bureau of Indian Affairs Chief William Johnson censured the embarrassed colonel. Despite his major gaffe, Bradstreet would still be remembered for his victory at Fort Frontenac. Moreover, the wealthy military man purchased ample land south of Albany, where he spent time with his wife and two children, when not pursuing other interests. He died at age 60 in New York City in 1774. That same year, the British Parliament passed The Quebec Act, which declared Ohio and lands in five other states to be part of Quebec. The act, never enforced, was repealed in 1791.

Skeptics may wonder how historians identified this spot in Rocky River as the location of the disastrous landing. In fact, it is documented in the diary of Captain John Montresor (Bradstreet's navigator), the letters of Sir William Johnson, the writings of historian Francis Parkman, public statements by Michigan Governor Lewis Cass in

1834, and the research of Dr. Jared Kirtland, a famed Northeast Ohio botanist and state legislator, in the 1860s. Additional evidence comes from random discoveries of swords, musket remains, a surgeon's knife, cannon balls, and a silver spoon, as well as old British and French coins, all discovered on the sandy beach over a period of many years.

Long before this stretch of beach became a city park, it was referred to as McMahon's Run and Hahn's Grove in recognition of families that owned the property. Their stories will come later in our book.

(One day in the late 1980s, a city employee at Bradstreet's Landing played a heroic role. Jim Harrington, an RRHS graduate, was on duty when he heard someone yell for help. Jim saw that the owner of a neighboring property, Jim Fitzgibbon – co-founder of Lesco Products or Lakeshore Equipment & Supply Company – had tumbled down the side of the hill in his backyard along with his tractor. Jim and a colleague called an ambulance, with one waiting with Fitzgibbon and the other guiding the rescue team to the site. Fitzgibbon recovered and lived for many more years, enjoying his family and his large private yacht. This is one of numerous stories of community heroism that are part of the Rocky River story.)

Bradstreet's Landing park was closed for a couple of years recently due to needed repairs, as the city implemented a $3.4 million modernization. The project included stabilizing the pier, combating erosion around Spencer Creek, building a new cabin, and improving the parking lot. The bait shop was permanently closed but the park is otherwise as beautiful and functional as ever. Now, further improvements are in the works including expanded parking and more seating areas for visitors' convenience.

A Grand Vision

Rocky River is now a quintessential suburb but more than 200 years ago, an ambitious pioneer named Gideon Granger became convinced that this area would become one of America's major cities. Furthermore, he believed he, his business partners and their families were the people who would make it happen.

To put this story into context, Connecticut in 1786 agreed to relinquish all claims to lands to the west except for a 120-mile area known as "the Western Reserve" that included Cleveland and Rockport Township (predecessor to Rocky River). The plan was for that state to sell off land in the Western Reserve to fund education and other state priorities.

Granger arrived in 1805. Following Bradstreet's 1764 disaster, some 40 years passed quietly and largely uneventfully in Rockport Township. To the east, in 1796, Moses Cleaveland and a team of 49 other individuals from the Connecticut Land Company surveyed the area that would later bear his name. A treaty was signed with Indian tribes to grant westerners title to disputed lands west of the Cuyahoga River in 1799. Those two steps were precursors to future development. Yet, when Ohio became the 17th state in 1803, Cleveland still had only a smattering of settlers.

In 1800, the United States had only four cities with more than 20,000 residents: New York, Philadelphia, Baltimore and Boston. All four cities had busy harbors which fueled Granger's futuristic thought process.

Granger was a trader, investor, land developer and future postmaster general but more than anything he was a visionary. From horseback, he saw a beautiful region with a navigable river, lakefront access and fertile soil. The area was heavily forested, inhabited by an abundance of wildlife, including deer, bears, wolves, turkeys, snakes, and other fauna. There was one narrow, established east-west path, used by Indians, roughly along the route of today's Detroit Road. Perched on his horse, Granger had grand visions of this undeveloped gem becoming a population center and an international shipping port. He envisioned it becoming known as Granger City.

Henry Canfield had purchased the 21-mile area known as Rockport Township, which included the future Rocky River, Lakewood, Fairview Park and points south. Canfield then sold parcels to interested parties. Granger accumulated land holdings that equated to about one-fifth the size of the current City of Rocky River. Along with his cohorts Joseph Larwell (spelled in some sources as Larwill), Calvin Pease and John Bever, he laid out plots for a city complete with a public square and advertised them for sale. In the meantime, he raised a family and promoted the area's future.

The initial results were encouraging, reinforcing Granger's confidence. Before long, 150 persons lived in the area and several small businesses were established. For example, Charles Miles bought land from Granger near today's Westlake Condominium, on which be built a log cabin that John James later converted it into a trading post-saloon.

A new path was cleared between 1810 and 1813 with state funding to allow easier stagecoach and foot travel from the Cuyahoga River all the way to the Huron River, a distance of 52 miles. This meant more traffic even if the passersby did not settle in Rockport Township.

The first grand wedding in what would become Rocky River is believed to have occurred in 1812. Chester Dean married Lucy Smith of Dover Township (Bay Village). Despite a snowstorm, a joyous reception was held. Chester Dean was still a major figure 22 years later, when he and his brother Samuel Dean purchased the southern part of Datus Kelley's lands and opened a tannery for transforming hides into leather.

Another early settler, Philo Taylor, arrived by boat in 1806. Following a verbal agreement with Canfield, Taylor built a residence on the Lakewood side of the river. Verbal agreements in lieu of a written contract have never been a good idea and this was a case in point. A dispute arose, with Canfield saying the land must be used for other purposes and that Taylor would have to choose another lot. Taylor angrily departed for Dover and was said to have put a hex on the entire area. Thereafter, every time some misfortune occurred, Taylor apparently took solace that his hex had been effective.

Dan Miner – another ambitious entrepreneur – moved into Philo Taylor's old cabin and ran a saloon. He also operated a ferry to help travelers cross the river and initiated construction of a mill operation. Sadly, Miner died in 1813, before his investment in any of these enterprises could flourish. His widow operated the ferry for some time thereafter. Miner's brother-in-law, Dr. John Turner, also lived briefly in the area until his house burned down. These events gave credence to those who chose to believe in the vicious power of Philo Taylor's hex.

One of the people who crossed the river on the ferry in 1812 is historically significant. His name was Valentine Ramsdell. This young man, about the age of 15, had joined his father and other volunteers and militiamen who went to the Marblehead peninsula to combat Indians who were attacking the settlers there. In September of that year, Valentine was captured by the Indians who scalped and dismembered the young man.

His father, Joseph Ramsdell, was wounded but survived. Valentine Ramsdell is remembered even today as a heroic volunteer.

Gideon Granger observed all of these developments with keen personal interest. Yet, economic hardships in 1817-1818 during the early years of the James Monroe Administration – coupled with the difficulty pioneers had in navigating from one side of the Rocky River to the other – slammed the brakes on development. The result was vacant cabins and unbuilt lots. It was a devastating turn of events for Gideon Granger who died fearing his dream of a grand Granger City might never be realized. One of his sons, John Albert Granger, turned his attention to the east side of Cleveland, which was growing faster. The son bought up land and encouraged development. Granger Road, which runs through a hilly section of Cleveland and Garfield Heights, is named after him. Another son, Francis Granger, inherited much of Gideon's original land holdings, which included acreage on both sides of the Rocky River, and sold off lots individually.

The concept of Granger City becoming an internationally important port city was never realized. Instead, Cleveland grew to be a prominent center for commerce and industry while Rocky River became a recreational center and eventually a quintessential suburb. And along that journey, many other fascinating people would play seminal roles as Rockport would become a bustling little township.

Becoming a Bustling Little Township

Today's Greater Clevelanders are familiar with suburbs such as Rocky River, Lakewood, Fairview Park and Middleburg Heights. Back in 1819, Rockport Township included these communities as one of Cuyahoga County's 19 original townships. Though there is no local city today called Rockport, the name is still referenced at The Shops at Rockport shopping center on Center Ridge Road and the Rockport United Methodist Church on Wooster Road.

Life was extraordinarily difficult in Rockport Township in the 1820s. Unlike established eastern cities, there were few established services. The purchase of imported goods was time-consuming and expensive. Self-sufficient families and neighbors relied on one another to make a go of it. Little by little, Rockport became a viable community. Here is what we know of some of the other early residents.

The History of Cuyahoga County by Crisfield Johnson notes that an elderly man named George Peake arrived with his family in about 1809, purchasing land on both sides of the Rocky River. Decades earlier, he had served in the British army. Peake, who was of mixed race, had married an African American woman in Maryland, and had several adult children. He and his family were free blacks, not runaway slaves. Mr. Peake was said to have been 105 years old when he passed away in Rockport Township in 1827. According to sources cited by the Rocky River Historical Society, other early landholders included Jeremiah Van Scoter, John Pitts, Benjamin Robison and Dyer Nichols.

Another memorable figure was an adventurer, businessman and industrialist named Datus Kelley. He and his wife Sara arrived in 1811 and bought a large parcel of prime real estate that ran from the lake south to Detroit Road. The eastern boundary of his property was today's Wagar Road and his property ran west to today's Bay Village. The price he paid is said to be just $3.18 per acre.

Figure 3 - Business tycoon Datus Kelley (public domain)

Kelley was a very headstrong – some might say stubborn – individual. He was an anti-slavery activist and an advocate of temperance. At Rockport's first township election in 1819, held at Rufus Wright's tavern, it's said that there were 19 voters and 18 offices to fill. Datus Kelley got Rockport Township temporarily declared a dry community. That status would not last for long since tavern owners relied on spirited beverages to serve to local residents and travelers alike.

Kelley operated a sawmill on his property – one of the area's first industrial businesses – near today's intersection of Detroit Road and Elmwood Road beginning in 1817. An unfortunate flood later put Kelley's sawmill out of business. He and his brothers also had an enterprise building docks for ships and boats.

Rockport Township was not Kelley's final destination. When the impatient businessman and his brother Irad Kelley learned of limestone deposits on Cunningham's Island (also known as Island Number 6 and Sandusky Island) in Lake Erie in 1833, Datus said goodbye to Rockport. He and Irad bought up land, parcel by parcel, until they owned the entire island. The enterprising pair opened a lucrative mining and timber-harvesting business and in 1840 legally changed the area's name to Kelley's Island, as it is still known today. Located 12 miles north of Cedar Point and four miles north of Marblehead, the island had been controlled first by the British and later by the United States in the War of 1812. General William Henry Harrison, a future U.S. President, made it one of his home bases for wartime military operations. Long inhabited before then by Native Americans, they had mostly left by the time of the war, making it ripe for settlement and industrialization. The Kelleys developed the island enough to ship limestone, lumber and fruit to the mainland. Kelley employed European immigrants and paid them sobriety bonuses if they abstained from alcohol. Ironically, his son-in-law, Charles Carpenter, opened a wine-making business there in 1842. Datus Kelley is buried in the small cemetery on Division Street on the island.

Back in Rockport Township, another Kelley son-in-law, Lucius Dean, built a home on the south side of Detroit Road in 1853. Incredibly, the Dean house was still standing until 1963, when it was demolished to accommodate the construction of the Oxford Court Apartments complex.

In 1831, two other families making their way from New York state to Ohio decided to travel together. After purchasing oxen and horses, they made the difficult journey, encouraging one another along the way. These two families also grasped the potential that Rockport Township offered. The McMahon family bought lakefront acreage that included the site of today's Bradstreet's Landing Park, resulting in the area being informally called McMahon's Run for many years. Their traveling companions, the Kennelly family, settled along today's Center Ridge Road.

One of the most influential of the early citizens was Rufus Wright, a veteran of the War of 1812, who arrived in 1816. He paid Gideon Granger the enormous sum of $300 for less than an acre of land near the river. Rufus operated a tavern for several decades on the site of today's Westlake Condominiums. His facility was two stories high with a large porch along one side, and a huge lawn area for socializing. Stage coaches frequently stopped at the property. Wright's Tavern doubled as the locale of public auctions and as the local Post Office. Rufus and his wife were a lively couple, making guests feel right at home with hospitality and storytelling. Wright's sons, Abraham, Philip and Frederick, also served as postmasters. There were several entrepreneurs operating taverns in the area at that time, but Wright had the greatest impact upon the burgeoning community. Wright spearheaded the financing and construction of the first bridge across the river in 1821, paying for half of the cost himself. His motivation was clear: Making it easier to get across the river meant more business for his tavern.

A father of six, Rufus Wright died in Rockport in 1856 at the ripe age of 84 and was buried in what was known as the Wright family cemetery. Today, that cemetery is beneath the parking lot of the old post office building on Wright Avenue, which is named for his family. (The Postal Service vacated the building in 1977 and it has been used for commercial purposes since then.) A cow-milking barn on Wright Avenue originally owned by the Wright family was said to have been standing for many decades.

The aging Wright sold his tavern to Jacob Silverthorn in 1853, who operated it for 23 years. Silverthorn, who was remembered as a congenial host, in turn, sold it to the Patchen family in 1876. The Silverthorn became known for serving delicious chicken dinners. This building would stand until about 1917, when it was torn down by members of the Bowles family.

Figure 4 - The Silverthorn shown in a postcard (courtesy of Harlan Radford).

By the 1850s, the term "suburb" was not yet in use. Yet, to all who observed closely, it was apparent that Cleveland was becoming the regional center of commerce and industry. In 1850, Cleveland had roughly 17,000 residents and was the nation's 41st largest city. Just 10 years later, more than 43,000 people were making their home in Cleveland, which was now the 21st largest city.

Gradually, Rockport Township was emerging as a destination for three categories of people – a) those who preferred a more rural setting for their daily lives; b) the wealthy who did business in Cleveland and wanted a second home in a bucolic setting, outside the congested city; and c) individuals and families who relished getting out of the city on weekends and summer vacations, renting a room at taverns or cabins.

Reuben Wood fit into that second category. He had a law practice in Cleveland and purchased his Rockport Township landholding from Datus Kelley in 1834, the year after Kelley left for his island business venture. Wood and his family loved nothing more than to escape on weekends to a more serene, lakefront setting. The fascinating story of Wood and his family is told in the next chapter.

Reuben Wood's Presidential Near-Miss

Reuben Wood was one of the most consequential of all residents of Rockport (later Rocky River). He served as a judge from 1833 to 1847. The life of a mid-19th Century judge was very different than today's jurists. Wood was constantly notified by U.S. Mail of cases to be decided. Rather than have the litigants come to him at his office in Cleveland or his second home in Rockport Township, Wood rode by horseback for hours and days at a time to various jurisdictions to hear and decide cases.

In 1850, Wood became the 21st governor of Ohio, and the first Democrat to hold that office in eight years (the Whig party had been in control). Moreover, for a brief moment in time, he was considered a leading contender for the U.S. presidency.

Figure 5 - Governor Reuben Wood (public domain)

To appreciate American politics in the day of Reuben Wood, it helps to look at the list of U.S. Presidents. From 1789 until 1837, every President served two terms except for

John Adams and his son, John Quincy Adams. Yet, after that, no President would serve two full terms until Ulysses Grant (1869-1877). Between 1837 and 1852, America had seen Martin Van Buren, William Henry Harrison, John Tyler, James Polk, Zachary Taylor and Millard Fillmore pass through the White House in rapid succession. None except Van Buren and Polk even served a full four-year term.

As the 1852 election approached, the Whig party nominated General Winfield Scott in lieu of incumbent President Fillmore. Democrats convened in June in Baltimore. The four major aspirants were Michigan Senator Lewis Cass, who had run on the Democratic ticket in 1848 and lost to Zachary Taylor; Pennsylvania's James Buchanan, who had been Secretary of State under President Polk; William Marcy of New York, who had been Secretary of War; and Illinois Senator Stephen Douglas, who would later become famous for his role in the Lincoln-Douglas debates. With four ambitious candidates – not to mention Texas Senator Sam Houston and several other longshot aspirants – the race was wide-open and hotly contested.

In such a scenario, some politicos and journalists envisioned a situation in which the party might choose a compromise candidate. Friends of Reuben Wood saw him as the ideal selection. On paper, he had an impressive resume as a current governor and a former judge. The Buckeye State had yet to become famous for producing Presidents (that would begin in 1868 with the election of Ulysses Grant) but Ohio was becoming an important state electorally. Moreover, Wood was tall, good looking and had a keen sense of humor, although he could also be crass and ungentlemanly.

The Democratic convention was a real donnybrook, requiring 49 ballots over four days and countless hours of political horse trading. How close did this Rockport Township resident come to landing the nomination? Wood was never formally nominated, and the official *Proceedings of the 1852 Democratic Convention* do not mention him. But contemporary sources reveal that he was seriously considered. A book titled, *History of Cleveland and Cuyahoga County,* written by Egbert Cleave, states, "The Virginia delegation then offered to the Ohio delegation to give the entire vote of Virginia to Governor Wood of Ohio if Ohio would bring him forward. The hostility of one man prevented this event." That individual is believed to have been the influential editor of *The Plain Dealer* newspaper. Democrats eventually nominated Pierce. Indeed, the Virginia delegation was the catalyst for Pierce's nomination. Months later in the general election, Pierce defeated Winfield Scott.

The election of 1852 was significant for a number of reasons. One was that the Whig party soon became a non-factor, and by 1856 the new Republican party had emerged as the alternative to Democrats. Second, although Pierce was elected President, he had a miserable time in office, was ineffectual on the major issues including slavery, and was out of politics four years later.

Wood was not interested in building a base to run in 1856. He loved his second home on the southwest corner of today's Avalon Drive and Wagar Road and affectionately called the home Evergreen Place. The home was white with green shutters, two stories on one side and one story with a covered porch on the other. He used the small log cabin on the property as a law office. When the family wanted to go for a summer swim, they simply walked to the beach (their path likely followed the ravine that still exists between two homes on Avalon Drive), shed their clothes, and waded into the lake waters. Wood planted trees on his property, some of which may still be present. Had Wood been elected President, Evergreen Place undoubtedly would still be standing as a major tourist attraction.

If there was a sense of dissatisfaction for Wood, it was that he had not accumulated massive wealth. In 1853, in a complete change of direction, Wood accepted an assignment from President Pierce and Secretary of State William Marcy to become American Consul to Chile. Wood welcomed this appointment as an opportunity to serve his country, quench his sense of adventure and profit from the collection of shipping duties. He took his family, including son-in-law George Merwin, who served as his secretary. (Merwin had built a gorgeous brick home in 1850 at 3028 Prospect Avenue in Cleveland that later became the Rowfant Club, a bibliophilic society. Merwin's home still stands and is designated a historic property.)

The sojourn to Chile was chronicled by a family member in an anonymously written book. Within just over a year, Wood and his wife were more than ready to return to Rockport and Merwin was appointed as his successor. (After returning to the States, Merwin remained married to Wood's daughter, but developed a drinking problem which is said to have made him miserable to be around. Merwin Avenue in the Flats in Cleveland is named for him.) Wood and his spouse enjoyed living at Evergreen Place for about 10 more years. At some point, he changed political affiliation. Previously a Democrat, he became an enthusiastic supporter of Republican President Abraham Lincoln. Wood died of bilious colic in October 1864, just days before he was to have co-hosted a rally in Cleveland for Lincoln's re-election. Wood is buried in Cleveland and his papers are property of the Rocky River Historical Society.

(Reuben Wood is the only Rocky River resident to become Ohio governor. Another Rocky River homeowner who had gubernatorial aspirations more than 130 years later was James Petro, who resided on Falmouth Drive with his wife Nancy and two children. Petro amassed an impressive resume as prosecuting attorney and city councilman for the City of Rocky River, Cuyahoga County commissioner, state legislator, state Auditor, and state Attorney General. He also worked in government relations for Standard Oil of Ohio. Petro sought the GOP nomination for governor in 2006 but lost in the primary election to Secretary of State Ken Blackwell, spelling the end of his political career. Petro now resides in Florida.)

Bridging the River

Nowadays, anyone wishing to cross the Rocky River by motor vehicle or foot can choose from among three bridges. But in the 19th Century, every journey involved either planning in advance how to cross the water or "crossing that bridge when one comes to it."

Imagine the experience of Reverand Joseph Badger and his companions who traveled from the east side of Cleveland to Rockport Township in 1801. Author Charles Whittlesey chronicled the journey in the *Early History of Cleveland Ohio: Including Papers and Other Matter,* quoting the clergyman as saying, "We swam our horses across the Cuyahoga by means of a canoe, and took an Indian path up the lake; came to Rocky River, the banks of which were very high, on the west side almost perpendicular. While cutting the brush to open a way for our horses, we were saluted by the song of a yellow rattlesnake, which we removed out of our way."

Ferry boats, when available, were only a temporary or intermittent solution. As history would unfold, there would be several different bridges over the Rocky River. Tavern owner Rufus Wright fronted half of the money needed to build the first bridge in 1821. His drive and determination ensured that the project was completed using local help. But his bridge was an imperfect solution. First, it was a low-level bridge that required negotiating one's way down a cliff on one side and up a cliff on the other. The muddy approaches were often treacherous. Yet, for 29 years, this bridge allowed stage coaches to cross the river, fostering the growth of Wright's hospitality business. This was one of the early examples of local citizens meeting a challenge through vision and determination.

The second iteration was a toll bridge built in 1850. Stagecoach accidents in the late 1840s convinced the Ohio Legislature and Cuyahoga County government to authorize the Rockport Plank Road Company to construct a toll bridge. Travelers now had to make their way up and down only one half of the height of the cliffs, since the bridge was built at the midway point between the top of the cliffs and the waterline. A muddy road leading to the bridge and a wooden toll house were located behind today's Westlake Condominiums. Assuming he had not dozed off, the on-duty agent would scamper over to the travelers and collect the fees.

A most unusual way to cross the river was to walk across a tightrope. A stunt man who went by the name Professor Jenkins – a forerunner of the Great Wallenda – did this in 1883, starting on the west near the Silverthorn Inn and crossing to the east side. Jenkins further girded his reputation on August 25, 1896 when he crossed the Niagara Gorge on a velocipede. Jenkins' great-granddaughter, Eileen Hall, was asked in 2012 if the tightrope talent ran in the family. Ms. Hall, by then 80 years old, replied no, and that she in particular was afraid of heights. Professor Jenkins' balancing pole and velocipede are on exhibit in a museum in Waterloo, Ontario.

The city of Cleveland passed the 100,000-resident mark sometime in the 1870s, and with more people living in Cuyahoga County, there was also more travel. Particularly during the summer, Clevelanders enjoyed getting away from the crowded and increasingly polluted city to the fresh air of the countryside in Rockport Township and points west. The county eventually took over operation of the 1850 bridge, which eliminated the tolls, but also led to neglect of the wooden bridge's condition. Complaints about the 1850 bridge grew.

Finally, an "iron bridge" was put into service in 1890. The third bridge across the river, this was an improvement in that it was built at ground level, but as the age of streetcars and automobiles approached, that conduit became obsolete soon after it was built.

That reality was never so clear as in 1905, when a westbound Lakeshore Electric Railway streetcar destined for Toledo came off the tracks, tilted sideways and broke through the protective iron railing. Miraculously, the rear wheels clung to the track, which allowed the heroic train engineer to rescue passengers to safety, even as part of the car was hanging perilously over the river below. Reflecting on that mishap and other concerns, a county government report declared that the iron bridge was unsafe. That resulted in a very different type of construction project that was completed in 1910.

The fourth bridge – often called the 1910 bridge – was at one time the longest span of unreinforced concrete in the world at more than 200 feet! So famous was this viaduct that it was pictured in school textbooks and on postcards that are still popular with collectors today. It was added to the National Register of Historic Sites. Built at a high level, this bridge was safer than its predecessors and was designed to accommodate every form of traffic, from automobiles to streetcars to horse-drawn vehicles to pedestrians. The bridge is front and center in the following postcard, which was U.S. Mailed to San Francisco in 1925. The railroad bridge is visible in the distance off to the right.

Figure 6 - The 1910 bridge carried automobiles, streetcars and pedestrians. (Author's Collection) Published by Braun Postcard Co., Cleveland, Ohio

The 1910 bridge enjoyed a much longer service life, but by the 1970s, engineering experts were warning that it was past its expected life span. After all, a bridge built during the William Howard Taft Administration could hardly be expected to still be in top condition during the Jimmy Carter Administration.

That reality led to the construction of the 1980 bridge that remains in service today, and the deconstruction of the 1910 bridge. Only one 175-foot portion of the 1910 bridge foundation remains, and an office building stands atop of it today. The accompanying photo shows the 1980 bridge-construction project in progress during a snowy winter, with the National City Bank sign to the left and the Westlake Hotel to the right.

Figure 7 - 1980 Bridge Demolition and Construction (author's collection)

The current railroad bridge was built in the early 1900s, slightly north of the 1980 bridge. Wide enough to accommodate double rails, it replaced an earlier single-track railroad bridge. From the Cleveland Yacht Club island, one can't miss the sound of trains as they ramble overhead.

Two other modern bridges have been built in the City to facilitate traffic across the river. In 1925, the Hilliard Boulevard bridge connected the southern parts of Lakewood and Rocky River. This fine bridge was constructed with non-union labor, which afforded a lower construction price. The bridge is in roughly the same location that a swinging walking bridge had existed until 1910. The swinging bridge was about 30 feet above the water level, composed of wood planks connected to strong ropes that supported the walkway. The Hilliard bridge construction project took a couple of years to finish and claimed one life. When completed, it was deemed worthy of a beautiful postcard.

Figure 8 - Postcard showing the Hilliard Boulevard bridge (author's collection)

The 1964 Clifton Park bridge connects Clifton Boulevard in Lakewood with Lake Road in Rocky River. Buses had replaced streetcars on Clifton Boulevard in 1947, but all westbound traffic, whether by bus or car, had to navigate over to Detroit Road or Hilliard Boulevard to cross the river, leading to traffic jams, delays, and citizen complaints. The Clifton Park bridge was built by the state to address those issues. As useful as the bridge has been for more than 60 years now, it was controversial at the time. Lakewood objected to the route, which required the purchase of several elegant homes as well as the loss of property tax revenue. A number of upscale Lakewood homes were relocated to vacant lots. Government officials in Rocky River had concerns about the bridge location, as well, though less vehemently held than those in Lakewood. In the end, the Clifton Park bridge was built over objections from both cities and helped smooth out traffic flows.

The First Churches

Rocky River today is home to an abundance of churches of diverse denominations that serve the spiritual needs of the community. This chapter looks at some of the early congregations, as well as the roots of current churches that are still bringing forth God's good Word in Rocky River.

The Rockport Methodist Episcopal Church, at 3300 Wooster Road, was built in 1847. It was not only the first church in Rocky River but is said to have been the first church west of the Cuyahoga River. The church organization traces its roots back to 1822. The 1847 building, which still stands, is a wooden edifice, with a parsonage next door. It's the oldest building of any type in Rocky River, and a testament to the religious conviction of early settlers in the young City. James Polk was the U.S. President at the time it was built.

Figure 9 - Interior of 1847 Church building at 3300 Wooster Road (courtesy of Zillow)

Through the years, Greek Orthodox and Romanian Orthodox congregations have also called that venerable building their church home. (The Romanian Orthodox parish relocated to Olmsted Township in 2012.) Meanwhile, Rockport Methodist Church continues to prosper. The congregation now worships across the street, on the east side of Wooster Road, in a larger and more modern building. Dr. Gordon Meyers was recently the senior pastor, succeeded now by Rev. Don Kraps.

Another early church was of the same denomination. The Rocky River Methodist Episcopal Church was organized in 1885 by a number of ladies who met together for worship mostly in a schoolhouse. Funds were contributed by generous donors including the wives of major landowners Clifton Beach and Daniel Eels, and the church building was eventually completed in 1893 at the corner of Detroit Road and Parsons Court, even amidst the national recession that year. The original design included a long shelter for buggies to keep the horses from getting too hot in the summer.

A fire in 1925 led to an expansion and modernization of the church, which was expanded again in the early 1950s after the parsonage was torn down. This congregation remains in operation in a 1957 Georgian Revival building with a tall, illuminated spire that can be seen as far away as Beach Cliff Boulevard at night. Rev. Daniel Bogre is currently the senior pastor.

Down the street to the west, St. Christopher Catholic Church followed in 1922. The church is named for a Third Century figure who is regarded as a martyr and the patron saint of travelers. Parishioners first met in the City Hall (Primett Building). The first church building suffered a fire just a couple of years after its construction in 1925. Following several expansions, it is now one of the larger Catholic parishes in northeast Ohio. The lead priest since 1997 has been Rev. John Chlebo.

The roots of St. Thomas Lutheran Church and School go back to World War II, when Rev. Otto Toelke was sent to Rocky River to knock on doors and canvas the area for a potential new church. He found a community hungry for Lutheran doctrine. The initial services were held in 1944 in a store at 2220 Wooster Road (between Shoreland Avenue and Riverwood Avenue). Later, the congregation met temporarily in another store on Lake Road (then Blount Street). The resourceful congregation bought three acres of vacant land at 21165 Detroit Road at county auction in 1945 and moved a small former schoolhouse from behind Beach School to the current location. A new church building – which is still in service – was constructed in 1959 to meet the needs of the congregation; the old schoolhouse was torn down in the early 1970s. Another expansion was completed in 1998. From 1994 until recently, the lead pastor was Rev. Eric Van Scyoc. The Rev. Jeremiah Jordan is now the "pastor sole."

West Shore Unitarian Universalist Church, located on Hilliard Boulevard, was founded in 1946. It held its initial services at Lakewood Masonic Temple. It purchased a tract

The First Churches

of undeveloped land on Hilliard in 1949 and the current building was erected in 1962. Rev. Anthony Makar is the senior pastor.

Rocky River Presbyterian Church was spun off from Lakewood Presbyterian Church in 1955. The congregation first met at Rocky River Memorial Hall while a new church facility was constructed on Detroit Road, west of the High School and next to a now-defunct business called Polly's Fruit Stand. The current sanctuary was completed in 1969. The first pastor was Rev. James Walker. Dr. Jon Fancher, a resident of Battersea Boulevard, was the popular pastor for half of the church's history, from 1991 until recently, squeezing in his pastoral duties while also working as a part-time actor and a school board member. At last report, an interim pastor was leading the services.

Figure 10 - Courtesy of Rocky River Presbyterian Church

The story of St. Demetrios Greek Orthodox Church goes back only to 1959. The northeast Ohio Greek community had a church on Cleveland's east side and sought one on the west side. For nine years, services were held at the old Rockport Methodist Episcopal Church at 3300 Wooster Road – the one built in 1847. This building was not large enough to accommodate the congregation, and was even less equipped to handle the bigger crowds at the annual church bazaar. In 1969, the congregation moved to a new facility on Center Ridge Road, near the border with Westlake. Many area residents look forward to the bazaar every summer, where delicious Greek food is sold. Some years, the festival attendance reaches as many as 40,000 people. The current priest is Father Andrew Lentz and the business manager is Byron Spooner, Jr., a former RRHS baseball and basketball star who also played minor-league baseball, before pursuing a career in business. His father, restaurant and funeral home owner Byron Spooner Sr., also was a parishioner before his recent death.

There is a small, quaint church building at 19147 Eastlook Road (formerly known as Helen Court), off of Wooster Road, that has been home to several churches. The edifice was built in the year 1900. Houses filled in the rest of the street around the church between 1910 and 1915, and the church seemed a bit out of place amidst a residential neighborhood. Originally, the church served the large community of Scandinavian immigrants and their offspring as Our Savior's Lutheran Church. Until the early 1930s, services were conducted in Danish. (Our Savior now worships at 20300 Hilliard Boulevard as Good Soil Lutheran Ministries, led by Rev. Marissa Harrison).

In 1951, Grace Baptist Church moved into the site on Eastlook Road. Grace Baptist had been organized in 1949 when a group of 16 believers prayed for formation of a church that would faithfully preach the Word of the Bible. It began holding regular Sunday services as well as inspirational evening revivals. Grace Baptist proposed to construct a new building in Rocky River in 1964 but it appears to never have been built. After Grace Baptist moved to a newer building in Westlake, Lighthouse Alliance Church occupied the century-old building until approximately 2018. The church building – one of the oldest buildings of any type in the city – still stands, and recently has been home to the Mighty Fine Floor Tape Company.

The First Church of Christ Scientist has occupied the lot across the street from Rocky River High School since 1950, three years after an organizational meeting was held in the Kensington School auditorium. The church features a reading room and a striking architectural design with red brick and a tall white spire.

A strong faith community helps anchor a city and its residents to a higher purpose and constructive morals, encouraging stability. Rocky River and the surrounding suburbs benefit from the good work done by these churches, their pastoral staff, and their volunteer leaders.

The Second Generation of Rocky River Businesses (1850 to 1900)

Rockport Township's earliest residents had moved west to find a better life. Upon discovering a beautiful, forested area blessed with a lakefront location, some stayed and made the developing area their home, while others kept traveling west to Toledo, Chicago and other growing cities, or south to locales like Columbus.

During the second half of the Nineteenth Century, most of the business development was in the eastern areas along Lake Road, Detroit Road and Wooster Road. The winter months were mostly about hunkering down and trying to stay warm, since central heat and snowblowers were just a figment of the imagination. But in the spring and summer months, there was not only productive agriculture but also a burgeoning hospitality industry that hosted parties and picnics. And as more people moved in and had children, businesses were needed to support those who were staying year-around.

Taverns played a central role in the lives of residents between 1850 and 1900. They were a place to share news and gossip, hear accounts from travelers, and hold community meetings. One of the popular spots was Rufus Wright's Tavern (later known as Silverthorn's and Patchen's). Other saloons operated as well, each within walking distance of one another for the convenience of those with a thirst to quench.

Much American history occurred during the years that Wright's Tavern stood. James Madison, the fourth president, was in office the year it opened in 1816, as the nation had recently emerged from the War of 1812. Franklin Pierce, the 14th president, was in the White House when Wright sold it to Jacob Silverthorn in 1853. Some 23 years later, Ulysses Grant was the chief executive when Silverthorn sold the property to the Patchen family in 1876. Then in 1884, during the Chester Arthur administration, Silverthorn repurchased the inn after eight years of doing business in Cleveland. The building would survive all the way until the time of Woodrow Wilson, the 28th president.

Famous aviators such as Amelia Earhart, Eddie Rickenbacker and James Doolittle overnighted at the Hotel Westlake in Rocky River, as did Admiral Richard Byrd, who claimed to be the first person to reach both the North and South Poles. Famed aviator

Charles Lindbergh also stopped at the Westlake, most likely to enjoy a meal or visit friends, though he is not believed to have lodged there. Another prominent guest in the Nineteenth Century was General Phillip Sheridan, the Civil War hero. Rutherford Hayes, the 19th President, was a resident of Fremont in northwestern Ohio. He too was a guest at the Silverthorn.

Frederick Wright, one of the sons of innkeeper Rufus Wright, owned 45 acres of land in Rockport Township and kept busy in the spring, summer and fall in the 1870s, 1880s and 1890s with raising and selling fruit and vegetables. His house was on Detroit Road, between today's Wright Avenue and Prospect Avenue. With more land than he personally needed, he also was a realtor, happy to accommodate those looking to purchase land if the price was right.

Calvin Giddings ran a wool-carding business (wool-carding involves separating and straightening sheep's wool so it can be used for making clothing). Giddings also took a turn as the local postmaster when the position was not held by members of the Wright family. Phinney's Corner at the intersection of Wooster Road and Center Ridge Road operated from the 1850s until Benjamin Phinney's death in 1864. For a time, the post office operated out of this location. F.S. Morley later operated a two-level general store at the same intersection in the 1890s and beyond. This intersection was important for another reason. There had been a long history of people crossing the river from the Lakewood side and walking up the path at today's Rockcliff Drive. After crossing the river, many travelers stayed at a nearby inn on today's Wooster Road. Those not already exhausted from their travel ventured further west and stayed at an inn at today's Clague Road.

An 1874 map shows the names of a number of Rockport residents and their family-owned business. These listings provide a sense of how early residents were making a living. An individual named A. Mastick was a postal clerk. J.W. Spencer, who owned land south of Center Ridge Road, was active in the brick and tile business. (A street in that area as well as a creek that runs all the way to Lake Erie bears his name to this day.) J.A. Potter was a bricklayer. C.W. Hall was listed as a fruit grower, as were C.W. Ranney and Smith Woodbury. Peter Smidt was listed as a grocer and proprietor of a hall suitable for wedding receptions. C.R. Jordan was a milk dealer and was presumably running cows in the area. Francis Wagar, a member of one of the region's best-known families at that time, was a realtor. John Granger was a farmer and stock dealer. H. Dreyer was a veterinarian surgeon. Andrew Warshing was operating a sawmill.

Finally, a gentleman named D. Dardinger was listed on the 1874 map as "proprietor of summer boarding at Tisdale Point. Boat landing and grounds in connection with accommodations. Picnics, excursions, etc." Tisdale Point was on today's Frazier Drive, overlooking Lake Erie and the Rocky River and was later the site of the Daniel Eels and Lee Wilson mansions.

The Second Generation of Rocky River Businesses (1850 to 1900)

Figure 11 - An 1874 graphic advertisement for picnics and excursions at Tisdale (Sunset) Point.

The attraction of summer outings warrants further explanation. By the 1870s, Cleveland was the nation's 15th largest city with a population that boomed from about 92,000 to more than 160,000 in the space of 10 years. Seven of every 10 Cuyahoga County residents lived in Cleveland proper. Once known as the Forest City, Cleveland industrialized, becoming a very productive city but also dusty, polluted and crowded. City streets had the pungent odor of horse manure. There is a natural human longing for nature and clean air, and it became harder for that need to be met in the congested inner city. Wealthy business owners and attorneys began building summer homes outside the city center. Those of lesser means could not afford to build a second home, but still wanted occasional access to the countryside, and places like Dardinger's mini-resort at Tisdale Point and the Silverthorn were popular locales for a few days of escape.

So, as time marched toward the start of the 20th Century, Rockport Township was increasingly being thought of as a resort destination as well as an agricultural community. In separate chapters, we will look at the fascinating evolution of Tisdale Point (Sunset Point) as well as the next generation of businesses in the early and late 20th century. But first, let's consider the impact of the railroads and streetcars in the evolution of Rockport Township and Rocky River.

Impact of the Railroads

From Ellicott City, Maryland to Pensacola, Florida, to Sparks, Nevada, there are dozens of American cities whose stories revolve around railroads. By no means was Rocky River ever regarded as "a railroad town." Yet, trains and streetcars played a meaningful role in the development of Rocky River and even today, if you look closely, you'll find a number of reminders.

The Civil War concluded in 1865 and the next 20 years were a time of frenetic track-building around the continent. It is sometimes said that one out of three American men during this era either worked for a railroad or in rail construction. If true, that is an astounding statistic. The nation was industrializing and freight traffic was growing at a remarkable rate. Passenger traffic was also at high levels, since the train was the most practical way to get from one city to another.

The Nickel Plate Railroad (also known as the New York, Chicago and St. Louis Railroad), was established in 1881. Its mission was to connect Buffalo, Cleveland, Chicago and eventually St. Louis by rail to compete with William Vanderbilt's Lakeshore & Michigan Southern line, which initially had a monopoly for some of those routes. The company adopted the "Nickel Plate" moniker after a Norwalk, Ohio newspaper called the company's planned railway "a double-track, nickel-plated railroad." It was a clever tagline and the phrase is still used to this day. The Nickel Plate's plan was to buy existing rail where it existed and lay new track where it didn't. It bought out the old Rocky River Railroad, or Dummy Railroad, which ran between Cleveland and the Lakewood side of the Rocky River.

Figure 12 - The Dummy Railroad was a short-lived passenger line as shown in this postcard (courtesy of Harlan Radford)

The owners built the first Nickel Plate bridge over the Rocky River in 1882, just a year after construction of the railroad commenced. The Rocky River train station on Depot Street was built the same year. The station, shown in the postcard that follows and the accompanying watercolor painting by Marilyn Phyllis, still is in use, making it one of the oldest existing structures in the city of Rocky River.

Impact of the Railroads

Figure 13 - The Norfolk & Western Train Station as seen in a 1970 postcard. (Courtesy of Harlan Radford)

Figure 14 - The Rocky River Train Station (watercolor painting by Marilyn Phyllis) (author's collection)

Ownership of rail lines changed hands with rapid frequency. Vanderbilt eventually purchased the Nickel Plate but steered most of the business to his other line. That meant the Nickel Plate was less busy, less profitable, but also capable of moving cargo swiftly. Vanderbilt's holdings were eventually merged with the New York Central. When the U.S. Justice Department determined that the syndicate of railroads affiliated with the New York Central violated antitrust party, the Van Sweringen brothers (who built the Terminal Tower in Cleveland) bought the Nickel Plate. They put an experienced railroad man named John Bernet in charge of the operations, and bought out another line with connections to Sandusky, Toledo, Peoria and St. Louis.

Rocky River was a natural choice for a stop on the Nickel Plate for a variety of reasons. A number of Cleveland business titans had summer homes in Rocky River, not the least of which was Daniel Eells, who later co-owned the Nickel Plate. From the train station on Depot Street, Eels could easily walk to his home at Sunset Point, or more likely be picked up by a horse-drawn carriage. There was also demand for freight deliveries, especially coal used by area businesses, including greenhouses, to power their operations. Building materials and U.S. Mail were also moved by rail. During these years, the train depot was a busy locale.

Electric streetcars became a viable commuter option in the 1890s and numerous lines were operated throughout greater Cleveland. The Lorain & Cleveland line opened in 1897 and used the 1890 bridge to cross the Rocky River. In 1901, the Lakeshore Electric operation, which was owned by Toledo Edison, absorbed several smaller lines, including the Lorain & Cleveland, and began offering streetcar transportation all the way from Cleveland to Toledo. In 1910, when the new concrete bridge over the Rocky River replaced the 1890 bridge, the streetcars began using the new, safer bridge. At this unique time in history, one could see automobiles, streetcars, horse-drawn vehicles, bicycle riders, and pedestrians sharing the bridge.

The streetcars made a large number of stops in Rocky River. After starting in Cleveland, the cars next traveled to what was called stop B, in Lakewood at the intersection of Sloane Avenue and Edanola Avenue. Today's small Sloane Park is near this point. At the time, Coulter's Drugstore, a short walk away, served as a ticket office. A poultry business was across the street from the drugstore. Streetcar stop one in Rocky River was by Wooster Road, just over the bridge. This stop was popular with those headed to the Silverthorn or other saloons. Stop two was on Detroit Road, where a flagman was employed to stop early automobile traffic as the streetcar approached. Stop three was at Linda Street, which to this day is a short span connecting Lake Road and Detroit Road.

From there, the streetcar went west down today's Ingersoll Drive and turned right (or north) on today's Smith Court, where it traveled underneath the Nickel Plate railroad tracks in an underpass built in 1897. Because the South Kensington neighborhood was not built until the 1940s, the streetcar was able to turn west toward stop four at Morewood Parkway.

The streetcar then ran down the center median of today's Beaconsfield Boulevard and paused at what was called stop six (there was no stop five), at the intersection of Wagar and Beaconsfield. A small streetcar facility with an interestingly sloped roof at this corner, built in 1908, remains as a 1,252 square-foot private residence at 715 Wagar Road.

Figure 15 - Former streetcar station at 715 Wagar Road (courtesy of Google)

From that stop, the streetcar proceeded through a right-of-way between the south side of Kenwood Avenue and the north side of Maplewood Avenue (which explains why homes in that zone have large back yards). It next paused at Elmwood Road, which was stop seven, and at today's Bradstreet Landing, which was stop nine. From there, it headed west toward other cities.

Those studying local history will sometimes see references to "the Rocky River freight terminal." This facility was actually in Lakewood, built in 1935 across from Coulter's Drugstore. Student groups and families took the streetcar from points west, disembarked at the Sloane station, and then crossed over to the freight terminal to pick up a train to League Park to watch Cleveland Indians games. United Van Lines later occupied the complex until 1963, when it was torn down to make room for the Mayfair Apartments (which also permanently closed in recent years).

Electric flashers were not installed locally on streetcar crossings until 1930. By then, the streetcar-era was in its twilight, as the automobile was becoming the king of the road. The Lakeshore Electric interurban streetcars ceased operations in 1938.

Meanwhile, ownership of the Nickel Plate Railroad passed to the C&O Railroad from 1937 to 1947. The Nickel Plate ordered a fleet of diesel electric Alco PA engines, as well as one last steam locomotive from the Lima Locomotive Works in Lima, Ohio. The last steam locomotive on the line was decommissioned in 1960. The Nickel Plate became part of the Norfolk & Western line in 1964, and the Rocky River train station gradually became known to local residents as the Norfolk & Western station. In 1982, Norfolk & Western merged with Southern to form the Norfolk Southern Railroad.

Back in the mid-1970s, Norfolk & Western was doing a lot of track maintenance in Rocky River, working out of the local station, even on weekends. In those days, the corridor still had two sets of track (one set was removed in the 1990s to achieve tax savings.) On one Sunday afternoon, a group of area boys of various ages with an interest in railroads spent part of their day observing the work and talking with the Norfolk & Western workers. The highlight of the afternoon came when an employee allowed one of the boys, John Corpus, who lived at 381 Cornwall Road, to throw the switch. It was a moment that all of the boys would remember for decades.

The volume of rail traffic going through Rocky River has ebbed and flowed over the years. Dennis Kucinich, who represented the area in Congress from 1997 to 2013, led a campaign to get some of the rail traffic re-routed to other corridors. These days, the traffic level is reduced. The Rocky River station includes some signal equipment and is home base for Norfolk Southern employees on the rare occasions they need to work on the tracks or the signals in the area. But the station is a vivid reminder of the role that trains and streetcars played in the growth of Rocky River.

Pottery Shards a Century Later

In 2013, a homeowner named Dominic Donnellan was digging in his backyard at 394 Riverdale Drive, near the Cleveland Yachting Club, to build a fire pit. To his surprise, he came across shards of pottery, buried deep in the soil. He eventually learned that the fragments trace back to the historic Cowan Pottery factory although it is unclear why they were found relatively far from the Cowan headquarters.

R. Guy Cowan opened the Cleveland Pottery & Tile Company in 1912 at 1360 Nicholson Avenue in Lakewood, near today's Corky's Place. After serving in the Army's Chemical Warfare Division during World War One, he returned to Lakewood, only to find that the gas well he had used to fire the kilns had become unproductive.

Cowan moved his studio and store in 1920 to Lake Road in Rocky River, which had a gas well on the property. (Many people today are surprised to learn that there were many gas wells in Rocky River, some operating past 1950. These were accompanied by tall metal towers, also known as flare stacks, to burn off unwanted natural gas.) One building on the property served as the gallery and studio. Cowan furnished a house to the west of the gallery for his parents. There was also an old barn that was used for packing and shipping.

He employed gifted ceramicists, some of whom lived nearby. One of his employees was Thelma Frazier Winter (1908-1977), who grew up in New Philadelphia, Ohio. She met Cowan at the Cleveland School of Art and worked with him from 1929 to 1931 before leaving to study at Western Reserve University. Becoming a renowned sculptor, enamellist and painter, she married fellow artist H. Edward Winter and the couple resided near University Circle.

Cowan employees tossed scrap items into the field south of the store and north of the railroad tracks. Local children enjoyed looking to see what they could discover. For a time, this business not only prospered, but gained national notoriety for its creative productions. At its peak, the enterprise had 10 buildings and employed about 45 workers, producing up to 175,000 wonders per year, sold by 1,200 stores and dealers.

Customers, who included future First Lady Eleanor Roosevelt and philanthropist Leonard C. Hanna, came from all over the nation and internationally to visit the gallery or place orders by U.S. Mail. Cowan produced a remarkably broad array of pieces, including vases, bookends, lamps, jars, and candleholders, as well as floor tiles. If you have ever viewed any part of the 1,100-piece Cowan pottery collection on exhibit at the Rocky River Public Library, or seen photos on the Internet, you can appreciate the beauty of Cowan's works of art.

Figure 16 - Part of the Cowan Pottery collection at the Rocky River Public Library.

The studio and gift shop remained open until 1931, when the financial pressures of the Great Depression rendered the business unsustainable. Cowan closed the business and went to work for the Syracuse China Company in New York. Howard Eells – the grandson of Rocky River landowner Daniel Eells – was appointed by the court to act as receiver/administrator for the company. After Cowan's pottery plant closed, the property was home to Barrett Creamery, which was a favorite place to go for ice cream and other frozen confections until it closed in 1958. The Barrett family still owns the property and operates a storage trailer business. Sadly, an original building was lost to fire in 2021.

Cowan – like so many prominent Rocky Riverites – is buried at Lakewood Park Cemetery in Rocky River. Fortunately, his legacy is kept alive not only through the museum at the Library, but also through an annual lecture series – the Cowan Symposium. In 2016, a historical marker was unveiled near Lake Road by Mayor Pamela Bobst and Bill Cowan, the grandson of the original proprietor. The marker is another reminder of this unique part of Rocky River history.

A Country Club and a Yacht Club

Many suburbs of 20,000 residents have neither a country club nor a yacht club. This quintessential suburb has both, and these fine clubs add to the city's prestige, quality of life and recreational diversity.

The Westwood Country Club was incorporated in 1914 by a group of local men who sought both a challenging westside golf course and a place they and their wives could kick up their heels and enjoy a social life. The founders included John Crider, John Hinz, John Kerlin, Robert Reid, Mort Weber, and John Zangerle. Their endeavor was not an instant success. Discussions about the need for such a club continued for some time before the needed financial commitments were made. Land that was being used as an apple orchard, vineyard and cabbage farm was purchased. The farmland was cleared and the course was built. When it opened, it was only nine holes and left some members wanting further improvements. The expansion to 18 holes required a second land purchase in 1917, and a new course was completed in 1926. The caddie program was introduced in 1931. Caddies receive extensive training and often look back at their time as Westwood caddies as a formative life experience and a valuable opportunity to interact with adults on the course. From 1955 to 1986, caddymaster Ernie Gottschalk is said to have trained and managed more than 4,000 caddies.

In 1929, men from Westwood won the first national championship in archery golf. This was a new game, developed in the 1920s, with the goal of shooting arrows into targets with the fewest number of shots. The swimming pool was added in 1950 and a pro-shop was built in 1955 to add to members' enjoyment.

The professional course record of 64 was set not surprisingly by golf legend Arnold Palmer in 1960 and still stands today. Baseball Hall of Famer Yogi Berra, entertainer Bob Hope and golf pioneer Bobby Jones have also played there, as have many of greater Cleveland's business leaders and sports figures.

In 1965, a fire broke out in a linen closet in the women's locker room. Staff quickly sought to vacate the building of visitors, but several stubborn men playing cards refused to leave until the card room filled with smoke. The damage was considerable and it took more than a year to rebuild a new and improved clubhouse.

Over the years, Westwood has been the site of thousands of golf outings, tennis matches, swimming lessons, casual dinners, weddings and parties. The current clubhouse was completed in 2009. Some families are now in their third generation of club membership. The apple trees near the 12th hole have been there for decades, a reminder of the rural setting on which the course was built.

Figure 17 - (Graphic courtesy of Westwood Country Club)

Westwood Country Club was not the first golf course in Rocky River. That distinction belongs to the Keswick Golf Club, which was in operation from approximately 1913 to 1916 in the Beach Cliff Number One community. The early course – the sixth in Cuyahoga County – started near Battersea Boulevard. The nine-hole course stretched almost to the location of Rocky River Park. Two golf pros who lived in a structure on the site helped run the course and assist golfers. A realty company had purchased the land from the Eells family heirs in 1907 with an eye toward residential development but the timing did not initially seem right from a financial point of view.

One of the golfers who enjoyed playing at Keswick was said to be Robert Rhoads, a native of Wooster, Ohio, who pitched for the Cleveland Naps from 1903 to 1909, according to a man quoted in the book *Rocky River Yesterday*. A profile of Rhoads from the Society for American Baseball Research indicates Rhoads spent a lot of his time during these years in Kansas City and later in California, so it's unclear how often he really played at Keswick. But it's entirely possible that he golfed there at least once while back in Ohio visiting friends and loved ones.

As demand for upscale housing near the lake grew, it became clear that this land could be put to a more lucrative use, and the Keswick course operations were discontinued. Many of the Keswick players switched their allegiance to either the Westwood Country Club or a course in Dover at the corner of Clague Road and Lake Road.

As long and proud as the history of Westwood Country Club is, the roots of the Cleveland Yachting Club (CYC) go back even further. CYC traces its history to the Cleveland Yachting Association (CYA) which was based in downtown Cleveland as well as the Lakewood Yacht Club which was headquartered in Lakewood near the east channel of the Rocky River.

The CYA was organized in 1878. Cleveland Mayor George Gardner played no small role in the organization's growth, serving as commodore for almost 16 years. A clubhouse was located at the East Ninth Street waterfront downtown, and the club operated from that urban location for nearly 20 more years. Eventually, as downtown Cleveland continued to industrialize, the club leaders foresaw a brighter future if they were to move west.

In 1914, the clubhouse was placed on a barge and moved to the large island in the Rocky River. This island, before becoming the summer destination for generations of boaters, had formerly been owned by a pair of businessmen named Dan Rhodes and Elias Sims. Two of the three engines owned by the Rocky River Railroad (or Dummy Railroad) were named after Rhodes and Sims, who were co-owners of that railroad. Rhodes also operated the Cliff House, a popular tavern and lodge on the eastern side of the bridge over the Rocky River.

Even earlier, one of the three islands that formed the current yacht club island was informally called "Dead Man's Island" because Indians had buried some of their dead there. The remains of skeletons were dug up numerous times, as recently as 1963 when the current clubhouse was being constructed. Prior to construction of the current facility, an earlier clubhouse was shown on the below postcard.

Figure 18 - An earlier CYC clubhouse as depicted in a postcard. (Courtesy of Harlan Radford)

Returning to the history of CYC, in 1895, George H. Worthington succeeded Gardner as commodore and continued to guide the organization's growth for 19 years. Worthington, who owned one the world's three largest stamp collections according to the Accessgeniology.com web site, was president of several businesses including American Chicle, the Cleveland Stone Company, and Union National Bank.

Meanwhile, the Lakewood Yacht Club had been founded in 1899 by A.J. Phelps and other boaters. One of Worthington's last acts as CYA commodore was to oversee the merger with the Lakewood Yacht Club in 1913, and to secure a paydown of the debt the latter organization had incurred in purchasing the island. When Worthington stepped down as commodore in 1914, the newly consolidated club had about 1,000 members.

During this era, aeronautic pioneer Al Engel used the yacht club island as home base for his "Bumble Bee" hydroaeroplane that could land on water. It was manufactured by the Curtis aircraft company, and Engel generated a great deal of publicity with his flights.

Through the decades, the leaders of the yacht club have persevered through a number of challenges, even as club members have enjoyed great seasons of boating nearly every summer. One challenge came after Worthington's tenure, when the club entered bankruptcy and emerged as a new legal organization. There was a clubhouse fire in 1925. The Great Depression in the 1930s took a toll on membership. A tragedy occurred in the mid-1970s in the form of a mid-day explosion at the gas dock on a sunny June day, taking the life of a club member, Jack Gould. The explosion could be heard many blocks away.

In the 1990s, winter ice blocks on the river that formed, melted, and refroze again, shown in the nearby photos, did extensive damage to the island, boat docks, many boats, and nearby properties. Once the cold weather abated, it took months of work to repair damage.

Figure 19 - Ice Jam on the Rocky River (author's collection)

Figure 20 - Ice Jam on the Rocky River (author's collection)

Alexander Winton was the commodore from 1908 to 1911. Winton was a prolific inventor with more than 100 automotive and bicycle patents to his name. He founded the Winton Motor Carriage Company, which manufactured cars, castings and other auto parts at 10601 Berea Road in Cleveland. Winton was recognized as making the first bona fide sale of an American-made automobile, and in 1903 made the first trip across the continental United States by car. The first all-American diesel engine was also made in his plant. The photo below shows one of his prize products, the 1910 Winton Six automobile.

Figure 21 - The 1910 Winton Six

Winton understood the value of publicity. In one photograph, Buffalo Bill Cody was shown posing in a Winton motor vehicle in 1904. Buffalo Bill was famous in North America and Europe for his entertaining shows that highlighted themes related to the old West, Indians, and the frontier. The early years of the auto industry saw rapid-fire innovation as well as a massive consolidation. A business slowdown in 1920 required the liquidation of much of the Winton company's assets, and in 1930 what remained became the Winton Diesel Division of General Motors. Winton owned a large lakefront estate in Lakewood, and in 1962, the Winton Place condominium was built on that land. His son, Alexander Winton, Jr., was the CYC commodore in 1941.

Other notable CYC commodores through the years (and what follows is nowhere near a complete list) included Lee Wilson, the founder of Lee Wilson Engineering Company, in 1943; his neighbor James T. Van Dorn, of the Van Dorn Iron Works Company, in 1947; Al Mastics, who penned the yachting column in the *Cleveland Plain Dealer* for decades, in 1957; and Herb Brugh, owner of several area restaurants including Herb's Tavern in Rocky River, in 1989. Dentist Bill Rudge who lived at the corner of Kensington Oval and Beach Cliff Boulevard., did the honors in 1979; John W. Kemper, the owner of Brost Foundry on East 55th Street and an Avalon Drive resident, was commodore in 1984. Manufacturers rep James W. Murray held the role in 1986 and businessman Charles M. Inglefield, who was the drummer in Michael Stanley's first band, The Scepters, was commodore in 1995. Jack Hunger, founder of World Shipping Inc., also served as commodore.

Figure 22 - Past Commodore Bill Rudge, left, with Joseph Kurkul on a CYC road trip in the early 2000s.

Members of CYC include many competitive and adventurous souls, including more than a few who have taken their time returning to port, even when lightning and thunder could be seen and heard in the distance. Many members have taken their boating interest to various parts of North America and other continents. Longtime member Clancy Shaffer was a golden gloves boxer and businessman who bought the *Minx* yacht from multi-millionaire J.P. Morgan in 1940. He was still having lunch and telling tales regularly at CYC in 2000 at age 96.

Then there was the Mercer family who lived at 21341 Aberdeen Road in Rocky River. Lovers of boating and Lake Erie, in 1966 they purchased the seven-acre Mouse Island (also known as Hat Island), near Catawba Point, from the descendants of President Rutherford Hayes. President Hayes and two other leading citizens from Fremont, Ohio, purchased the undeveloped island in 1874 from Ira Dutcher of Catawba. Hayes eventually bought out the co-owners. Hayes' family built two cabins and a tennis court and used it as a perfect island getaway. Hayes died in 1893 and as family members gradually left Ohio by the 1930s, the island fell into neglect.

The Hayes family owned it all the way until 1966 when Rocky River's adventurous Mercer family bought it. The Mercer's enjoyed camping and exploring for remains on the island. Long owned by the three Mercer brothers – Bill, John and Buck – it is largely undeveloped even today. Ottawa County public records show that the island was sold in 2024 to an entity titled Mouse Island Yacht Club. For three decades, an annual sailboat race sees boaters sail around the island.

Figure 23 - Mouse Island in Lake Erie

Racing occurs virtually every summer weekend off the shore of Rocky River, but in 1990, CYC hosted a special race – the Star World championship regatta. This event moves around the world each year. Al Wismar was the commodore that year, and months of committee preparation went into the planning and execution of the races and the accompanying celebrations. Presenting this huge international sailing event was a true honor for the local yachting community.

The yacht club island itself was originally part of Lakewood but was legally transferred to Rocky River in 1946. The change made sense since the access point to the club – Yacht Club Drive – is in River, and the Lakewood police, fire and services departments had to leave city grounds every time they drove to the club.

Access from the mainland to the CYC island is via a bridge. The current bridge dates to 1987. The clubhouse was built in 1963 and has been modernized and redecorated numerous times. The swimming pool, at 50 by 100 feet, is another major attraction. Boats of all types and sizes are docked on the north, east and west sides of the island.

During the late 1960s and early 1970s, it was common to see the large yacht Gemini docked on the Lakewood side of the east channel. Gemini once belonged to the

A Country Club and a Yacht Club

flamboyant Duke of Windsor (that name might not mean much to most people today, but he was quite the public figure in the mid-20th Century). By the 1960s, Gemini was owned by Vernon Stouffer, the Cleveland Indians owner and president of the Stouffer foods and hospitality empire.

The two small oil paintings below depict a boating scene from the Rocky River. They are signed by the painter although it is difficult to discern the name with certainty.

Figure 24 - Paintings of the Rocky River (author's collection)

Through the years, not just CYC members have been attracted to boating or been drawn into the maritime scene in one fashion or another. Others have, as well, with a couple of interesting stories to follow.

By the 1940s, there were many business leaders with interests in efficient shipping of cargo on the Great Lakes. Senator Robert LaFollette of Wisconsin proposed a bill in 1944 that called for new regulations on this shipping activity. A 1944 U.S. Senate Commerce Committee document lists a large number of northeast Ohio businesspersons declaring their opposition to these changes, arguing that the bill would result in delays in the delivery of shipments and increased litigation in the courts. Among them were several individuals residing in Rocky River: Banker R.L. Williams of 21177 Kenwood Road; banker A.H. Bennett of 21130 Kenwood Road; banker A.E. Mason of 56 Oak Road; and investment banker W.S. Brown of 240 Cornwall Road (this author knew Mr. Brown's widow when he was growing up in the 1960s. The same home was later owned by Dan and Patty Ward who were big fans of Elvis Presley).

Figure 25 - Home at 240 Cornwall Rd. once owned by banker W.S. Brown (courtesy of Zillow)

Back in the 1960s, Jere Roach of 19002 Westhaven Lane in Rocky River enjoyed making boats as a hobby. The September 2, 1964 *Cleveland Plain Dealer* ran a photo of Roach, his wife, and four-year-old daughter Judy (a future 1978 RRHS graduate) in their pontoon catamaran sailboat which had two hulls and a trampoline in the center. According to Mr. Roach, their craft was twice as fast as a sailboat and more fun to operate!

One of Greater Cleveland's most accomplished seamen was Newman Christian Larsen (1903-1988), a resident of Rocky River. As a child, he helped City employees plant trees on Wright Avenue and Prospect Avenue. As an adult, he became the captain of the Edmund Fitzgerald ship.

Figure 26 - The Edmund Fitzgerald freighter (courtesy of Greenmars CC BY-SA3.0)

Larsen retired in 1969, six years before the ship's ill-fated sinking on November 10, 1975 on Lake Superior, which was later memorialized in a Gordon Lightfoot song. All 29 crew members died in the tragedy. For the rest of his life, Larsen enjoyed seeing the trees that he had personally helped city workers plant decades earlier. Newman Larsen is buried at Lakewood Park Cemetery in Rocky River.

Military Matters in Rocky River

There is no military base in Rocky River but as the U.S. military has evolved, some of the manifestations of those changes have been visible in parts of the City. These true stories only add to the historical appeal of this quintessential suburb.

Residents now think of the west channel of the Rocky River in terms of recreational boating and waterfront housing. But back in 1917, the Rocky River Dry Dock Company was building yachts and military vessels. The Hotel Westlake had yet to be built, and this small shipyard was in what would have been the hotel's back yard. Equipped with electricity, a blacksmith shop, and modern power tools, the company built several submarine chasers for the congressionally authorized Emergency Fleet Corporation. The chasers were later used by the French military. Subchasers were wooden boats, approximately 110 feet in length, that could be constructed quickly by knowledgeable craftsmen. Each was powered by three six-cylinder engines. Across the United States, many subchasers were built by small companies, such as Rocky River Dry Dock. The boats could move at high speeds and often traveled in groups of three to carry manpower and supplies while keeping lookout for German U-boats. Their wood construction was less likely to trigger explosives in the mine-infested waters than steel ships.

At its wartime peak, Rocky River Dry Dock had about 200 employees. According to the book *America's Maritime Progress* by George Weiss, the company was led by shipbuilder Theodore Zickes, later by Captain N. Simonson, and then by C.E. Kyle (a vice president at the Rocky River Savings & Banking Company) after Simonson's 1917 death. One can only imagine the scene – 200 craftsmen and carpenters making their way to the eastern-most point of Rocky River, knowing they were producing boats that would play a role in the Great War.

Around the same time, CYC opened a summer Naval & Recreation School to boys ages 9 to 18. It was an overnight camp that lasted for six weeks, with cadets engaging in fitness improvement and military-like drills during the day and sleeping in tents on the island at night. This program was an early forerunner of CYC's co-educational sailing camp program, which has focused on recreational boating, swimming, and water skiing, in later decades.

Toward the end of World War I, according to author Sunny Christensen, the Army Battery B artillery unit was stationed in the MetroParks valley, near today's Lakewood filtration plant. Their assets included barracks, stalls for horses, cannons, and other equipment. They often held detailed drills on the land owned by the Schlather family near Wooster Road in Rocky River. The considerable amounts of dung generated by their horses were purchased by the Christensen family for use as fertilizers at their farm and greenhouse complexes. According to Christensen, the Battery B outfit was disbanded in 1938.

In the mid-1940s, the U.S. Army worked with the Bell system to develop anti-aircraft technology that was named Nike after the mythological goddess of victory. Once the technology was in place, it was deployed in sites around key metropolitan areas in the 1950s. Because of its industrial base and transportation resources, Cleveland was one of the areas chosen for such elaborate and carefully planned protection. A series of Nike sites were constructed in Bratenahl, Painesville, Willowick, Warrensville Heights, Garfield Heights, Parma, Burke Lakefront Airport, and Fairview Park/Rocky River. A command center was based at the Shaker Heights Armory.

The Fairview/Rocky River Nike site was activated in 1956 with a battalion of military officials to staff the site. The launch base was said to be at 21700 Westwood Avenue near Westlake. The site included missiles, underground missile storage and launchers, a fueling area, a launcher-control station, military barracks, mess hall and administrative office. Ajax missiles were replaced with more sophisticated Hercules missiles at the base in 1959.

The technology quickly became obsolete and this base was one of the last to be fully decommissioned as part of arms-control agreements with the Soviet Union in June, 1971. For 12 years until 1983, ownership remained with the 135th Military Police unit. Today, the land from the old Nike site is now Tri-City Park, on the border of Rocky River and Fairview Park near Westlake. In a bit of irony, local residents now can be seen wearing Nike shoes while playing tennis and basketball at the former Nike site.

During World War Two, a presidential executive order from President Franklin Roosevelt established the Petroleum Administration for War program. One of many dozens of FDR initiatives that expanded the powers of the federal government, the aim was to allocate available supplies of petroleum products to the highest-priority purposes. The nation was divided into six regions, each of which had an administrator to collect and process data, as well as make allocation decisions. The program was in effect from 1942 to 1946.

One of the key figures in this endeavor was a resident of Rocky River. W.W. Vandeever had graduated from Southern Illinois – Carbondale University and was president of Allied Oil Company. His expertise made him an excellent choice to be the Petroleum Administrator for War for 15 states. He executed these responsibilities and further polished his reputation as a wise leader. Even after the conclusion of the war, U.S. congressional committees called on him for his expert testimony in Washington.

Vandeever and his family resided at 21621 Avalon Drive. In June 1950, Vandeever received the first-ever Honorary Doctorate degree issued by his alma mater. He is buried in Lakewood Park Cemetery. His descendants continued to live in Rocky River many years thereafter.

Neighbors to the East: Lakewood

Rocky River is bordered by several other fine communities. There are inescapable historical, cultural and commercial links between the cities. Across the river to the east, Rocky River is bordered mostly by the Metroparks system, the City of Lakewood and a small area bordering Cleveland. Once part of the original Rockport Township along with Rocky River, Lakewood is a 5.6 square mile jurisdiction. Established in 1889, Lakewood is a larger, diverse suburb with many business centers and long-established neighborhoods.

The old Indian path that evolved into Detroit Avenue became the center-point for residential and commercial development in the 19th Century. Mail was carried along that path by horseback-riding delivery personnel and later by stage coach. James Nicholson was said to be among the first permanent settlers in 1835, ignoring warnings from his contemporaries that Indian tribes would make it an inhospitable place to settle. Early landowners such as Mars Wagar and naturalist Dr. Jared Kirtland helped drive early development efforts. The nationally known Kirtland built his home at 14013 Detroit Avenue in 1839 (where it stood until it was flattened a century later to make room for a Kroger's supermarket).

Land was put to use for homes, orchards, vineyards and farms. Saloons were opened to provide for socializing and libation. Planks were placed along Detroit Avenue to make an easier ride for horse-drawn transport and until 1901, tolls were collected for transit across the improved road. Schools were opened to offer a bright future for youngsters. A municipal electric plant was built in 1896 to supply power throughout the community. A water plant provided clean drinking water not only to Lakewood residents, but later to those of Rocky River, as well.

At the dawn of the Twentieth Century, Lakewood was still a small town with only 3,355 residents. Growth soon accelerated, owing to its lakefront location and proximity to Cleveland, which was becoming one of the nation's 10 largest cities. Also fueling growth was the 1917 construction of the Detroit-Superior High-Level Bridge in Cleveland. This bridge better connected Lakewood with Cleveland's near west side, downtown, and well-developed east side. By 1930, the Lakewood population had exploded to 70,509 and the city was considered an upscale housing option with easy access to downtown.

That 1930 census proved to be the city's high-water mark. Since Lakewood was already largely built out by the time the Baby Boom began, the construction focus shifted to apartments. The resident count dipped slightly off and on for nearly 40 years, before rebounding to 70,131 in 1970. It has declined steadily since then, and as of 2023, Lakewood was estimated to be home to just over 49,300 people.

The oldest stone house in Lakewood was built in 1834 on the north side of Detroit, east of the corner with Warren Road. It was a private residence until 1899, when it became the home office for the Lakewood Realty Company. Various tenants – mostly commercial businesses – followed, including a furniture repair shop run by Gilbert Hostelley, from 1919 to 1952. Finally, in 1953, with the stone house increasingly out of place within a busy urban corridor, it was put on wheels and moved to its current location in Lakewood Park, on the site of the former 97-acre estate of John Honam, who was a weaver. The house is now a museum under the auspices of the Lakewood Historical Society.

William Maile took advantage of Lakewood's rich soil to operate a brickyard in the early 1900s on Hilliard Boulevard at Warren Road. The Lakewood Engineering Company employed more than 300 people on Berea Road. Lakewood even had its own automobile plant, as Templar Motors made cars from 1917 to 1924 at 13000 Athens Avenue at the intersection with Halstead Avenue. Part of the 18-acre complex remains today as an industrial center and the Screw Factory, which is now a large events center and artists loft.

Another example of manufacturing was the National Carbon Company, at the corner of Madison Avenue and West 117th Street. The company, which in the 1890s manufactured batteries and gas masks, was a major employer, but it suffered from a lack of public transportation. Its solution was to develop a self-sufficient neighborhood, complete with housing, parks, gardens, eight churches, and retail stores. By 1910, an estimated 2,200 people lived in the neighborhood, which came to be known as Birdtown. Many were National Carbon employees who walked back and forth to work. National Carbon became known as Union Carbide and is now owned by Dow Chemical. Neograf Solutions occupies the old National Carbon location today.

Once the population began to surge, major business corridors filled in along Madison Avenue and Detroit Avenue. Entrepreneurs stepped forward to fill the need for grocers, bakeries, hardware stores, tailors, shoe repair, law offices, banks, funeral homes, restaurants, and movie theaters. Today's Beck Center for the Performing Arts on Detroit was formerly the location of the Lucier Theater. The Lucier opened in 1927, and in 1937 was reconfigured for live theater, dubbed the Lakewood Little Theater. Further south, the Lincoln Theater on Madison and the Hilliard Square Theater on Hilliard, drew movie-lovers from around the area including Rocky River, as did the Detroit Theater at 16107 Detroit Avenue.

Even as Lakewood's civic leaders were cultivating the image as a great place to live and raise a family, they had mixed feelings about Scenic Park, an amusement park established in 1895 in western Lakewood near the river. The privately owned park featured amusement games, boat rides, a baseball field, dance hall, scenic railway ride, and restaurant. There also was plenty of alcohol consumption, drunkenness, rowdyism, and fights that sometimes spilled out into the neighborhood and the streetcars that took people to and from the park. Lakewood voted to become a dry community, but park attendees still accessed alcohol by walking on the nine-foot-wide footbridge over the river to today's Rocky River, where spirited beverages were sold. Eventually, Lakewood shut down access to the footbridge, took over the park lease, and rebranded the locale as Lincoln Park. Although new family-oriented attractions were added, a dry amusement park just wasn't as much of a draw. Park attendance plummeted and operations were ceased. Neighbors rejoiced as their peaceful neighborhood returned to normal. Lakewood bought the land in 1917 and donated it to Metroparks in 1925.

The intersection of Detroit Avenue and Warren Road became one of the city's busiest urban intersections early in the 20th Century. The late 1880s Victorian home of Francis Wagar (son of longtime resident Mars Wagar) and other older structures were leveled to make room for the new commercial interests, including the Bailey's Department Store which opened its Lakewood store in 1930. It's a shame those classic Victorian homes no longer stand but they gave way to inevitable commercial progress.

Lakewood's Independence Day celebrations and fireworks shows were always popular with people from Rocky River, since the latter community did not often have a show on July fourth. The parking lot at Lakewood Park would quickly fill up, and visitors had to park alongside neighboring streets. Lakewood residents would barbecue and hang out on their front porch and then stroll over to the park to see the pyrotechnics, or watch them from their back yard.

The shows were always well attended, but the 1982 event was memorable for a different reason. The fireworks misfired right from the get-go, with sparks being sprayed directly into the crowd, burning holes into the clothing of numerous attendees. No public announcement was made, but the stunned crowd quickly concluded that the show was over when no further pyrotechnics were lit.

With its diverse business interests, Detroit Avenue in Lakewood has always been a short, enticing bicycle ride for youngsters from Rocky River. In the 1970s, it was common for teens from Rocky River to make the trip to visit the Lakewood YMCA, Kovac's Comic Books and Baseball Cards shop, Daffy Dan's T-Shirts, the Daystar Boutique, a used records store, and Wing's Hobby Shop. The latter store operated from 1947 to 2014 and was a great destination for model railroad supplies, toy rockets, model cars and planes, and various games. When the hobby shop finally closed after 67 years, the owner said young people were no longer his best customers. When it was parents and grandparents who were the base of a declining business, he knew it was time to close up shop. Yet, even today, Lakewood attracts many Rocky River residents for everything from bars, bowling, and restaurants to doctors' and lawyers' offices.

Public schools in Lakewood were named after prominent Americans such as Abraham Lincoln, Ralph Waldo Emerson, Rutherford Hayes, James Garfield and Horace Mann. As the population declined after 1970, there was less need for schools. Taft Elementary School, named for William Howard Taft, was shuttered in 2008; and the 100-year old Franklin School, obviously named for Benjamin Franklin, was closed in 2009. The McKinley Elementary School, named for William McKinley, was destroyed in 2014 (giving way to new townhomes). The same trend carried over to churches. Amidst a public uproar, historic St. James Catholic Church was closed in 2010 by the Cleveland Catholic Diocese, despite the fact that 4,500 people were worshiping there.

Though decades have passed, the diverse neighborhoods and mix of Victorian, colonial and Tudor homes, are ever-present reminders of Lakewood's original monikers – "City of Beautiful Homes" and "Cleveland's Fashionable Suburb."

Clifton Beach's Life and Legacy

From Lakewood, let's turn back to Rocky River, and the northern area between Detroit Road and the lakefront.

Clifton Beach was an industrialist, attorney, real estate investor, deputy collector of customs in Cleveland, and Ohio congressman who lived a relatively short but impactful life. He was the son of a physician and his only surviving sibling was brother Ed Beach, a Bay Village resident who owned the K.D. Box Company.

Figure 27 - Congressman Clifton B. Beach of Rocky River (public domain)

Having graduated from Western Reserve College in 1871, Clifton practiced law for more than a decade. He married Janet Chisholm, daughter of industrialist Henry Chisholm, the chieftain of the Cleveland Rolling Mills Company, a massive iron-rail and steel producer that at its peak had 8,000 workers. Now incredibly wealthy thanks to the marriage, Clifton went into business with his in-laws on a manufacturing firm – the H.P. Nail Company. The company started out making nails for horseshoes, which was not especially profitable. Once they expanded into staples, construction nails, and rods, the company became one of the largest businesses of its type.

Socially, Beach was a member of the Union Club and the Roadside Club of Cleveland. Generous as an entertainer, his guests included William McKinley and Marcus Hanna, two of the nation's leading political figures. Clifton's first wife, Janet Chisholm Beach, died in 1890. He remarried in 1897, tying the knot with Adelaide Dixie Thaw of St. Louis.

Beach was allied with the Republicans and after the U.S. economy tanked during the Panic of 1893, Beach decided to run for Congress and try to make a difference. He was elected in 1894 and served two terms. Given his interest in industry, it's not surprising he was assigned to the House Committee on Manufactures. He was also a member of the Committee on Election of the President, Vice President and Congress.

As a junior member of Congress, Beach did not wield great influence. That was reserved for senior members like House Speaker Thomas Reed of Maine and Republican Conference Chair Charles Grosvenor of Ohio. The Library of Congress supplied this author with a list of all of the bills that Beach introduced. Many of them pertained to pardoning military deserters and providing federal pensions to certain individuals. During his time in office, he missed more than 60 percent of the votes. It is unclear whether it was business concerns, health matters, or the desire to spend time with his new love interest that kept him away, but in those days it was not uncommon for lawmakers to miss a lot of votes. He did not seek another term in 1898 and returned his focus to his business interests. His congressional seat remained in GOP hands until the 1912 election.

Beach was a shrewd investor. Back in 1888, he purchased 427 acres of prime Rocky River lakefront land in two parcels from the surviving daughters of Ohio Governor Reuben Wood. He then owned nearly all of the beachfront property in the city, save for the Oakwood Estate owned by Daniel Eells. Beach lived in George Merwin's former house in Rocky River, which he remodeled and redecorated. He also donated a parcel of wooded land along Detroit Road for Beach School.

Figure 28 - Beach School (courtesy of Rocky River Public Schools)

One of the oldest current structures in Rocky River, dating back to 1848, is at today's 21565 Aberdeen Road. Set back further from the road than most of the street's homes, Beach leased the house to Albert DeForest (1849-1908), a friend and colleague from the nail factory. By the 1960s, the aging edifice appeared to be in disrepair but it has since been updated and boasts a tremendous curb appeal as shown in the photo below.

Figure 29 - 21565 Aberdeen Road (courtesy of Zillow)

There is some baseball history associated with another house still standing at 21530 Lake Road, which dates to 1890. It was a country home of future Cleveland baseball owner Charles Somers, who was influential in starting the American League in 1901. Somers was a coal-industry executive in Cleveland who enjoyed weekend retreats to Rocky River and to Put-in-Bay, where he passed away in 1934. This five-bedroom, six-bath house (shown below) is still a private residence and a plaque on the home references its history.

Figure 30 - House dating to 1890 was summer home to a founder of baseball's American League (author's collection)

William McKinley became the second of the U.S. Presidents to visit Rocky River (Rockport) (after President Hayes). He was in the area, accompanied by Senator Marcus Hanna, to visit Congressman Beach, and saw Beach's large landholdings along today's Avalon Drive. (Richard Nixon is said to have been the third, visiting Westgate Mall in 1960 while serving as Vice President and campaigning for the White Houe. In 1972, President Nixon appeared in a motorcade starting at Hopkins Airport but did not visit Rocky River or Fairview Park.)

Beach died in Rocky River at age 57 in 1902 and his widow relocated to New York City where she lived 38 more years. The land was farmed with underwhelming results until his estate sold most of the land in 1917 to Realty Underwriting Company. The once grand Merwin-Beach home was vandalized repeatedly and finally burned to the ground in 1923. Clifton Beach's son, Chisholm Beach, showed little interest in Rocky River. He was seemingly enjoying a wonderful life until he died prematurely at age 36 in 1918 in a New York City subway. He was a three-time golf champion at the New York Athletic Club and worked as a vice president of the Calculating Company of New York. Different sources cite a heart attack or a stroke as the cause of the young man's death.

A developer built out the Beach Cliff Number One and Number Two neighborhoods, holding in reserve lots for the Wagar Beach park and another small park by Parklawn Drive. Construction materials in the early days of homebuilding were brought in on horse-drawn carts. Englishman Alfred Smith, hired by the developer, laid out the street plan. Smith drew heavily on his homeland with British road names such as Falmouth, Kensington, Stratford, Beaconsfield, Aberdeen, Avalon, Buckingham and Arundel. Clifton Beach is buried in Cleveland's Lakeview Cemetery. Nearly 120 years after his death, Beach Cliff Boulevard, the Beach School building, remnants of a stone wall at Beach School, and Wagar Beach all remain as reminders of this remarkable man's life.

Daniel Eells, Lee Wilson and Sunset Point

Daniel Parmalee Eells never served in Congress, and never had a street named for him, so he is less well remembered than Clifton Beach. But Eells was another prominent Clevelander who left an imprint on Rocky River.

Eells was the president of Commercial National Bank of Cleveland from 1868 to 1897 and was a director of 32 industrial and railroad companies. Those roles allowed him to accumulate considerable wealth. Eells was the owner of a grand home at 3201 Euclid Avenue on the famed "Millionaire's Row" which at its peak featured 300 mansions. The Eells mansion on Euclid stood until 1959 when it was sadly razed to build a motel. President-Elect James Garfield was among the guests at Eell's daughter's wedding at that mansion. President Ben Harrison, the 23rd chief executive, visited Eells in Cleveland sometime later. Some historians believe that it was in the library of Eells' Cleveland home that Eells and Senator Marcus Hanna convinced William McKinley to make his successful run for president. A book by Karl Rove, "The Triumph of William McKinley: Why The Election of 1896 Still Matters," provides great insight into the election of 1896 for those interested.

Eells also was a civic benefactor. In 1881, Eels, J.H. Wade and W.S. Streator conveyed 25 acres on Euclid Avenue to establish a campus for Case University. The three were trustees for the burgeoning institution. A committed Christian, Eells was also president of the Cleveland Bible Society.

Eells and his wife purchased 69 acres – formerly the Erastus Tisdale and Owen Moore farms – including Sunset Point, the most dramatic vista overlooking the river and Lake Erie. His property ran westward to today's Falmouth Drive; and from Lake Road north to Lake Erie. The main entrance to his estate was under the rail crossing at today's Beach Cliff Boulevard, a railroad that Eells co-owned. The stone wall remnants there, and on Lake Road across from Bearden's Restaurant, date back to 1892, marking the exterior of his property. Eells was also a yachtsman. He was the first owner of the *Winifred,* a massive 89-foot steam yacht that he purchased in 1882. Eells sometimes used it to travel between Rocky River and Cleveland. According to a database maintained by Bowling Green State University, he owned it until 1892, when he sold the vessel to Henry Ledyard and the Russell brothers, George and Henry. Ledyard was the grandson of former Michigan Governor/Senator Lewis Cass, and the son of the

Detroit mayor who shared his name. The ship was decommissioned in Sandusky in 1908.

Sadly, his Rocky River home overlooking the lake burned to the ground, attributed to a curtain being ignited by a gas flame. At the time Rocky River lacked an organized fire department. Eells and his wife built a Victorian home a bit further inland, at 19715 Frazier Drive, at the corner of today's Frazier Drive and Oak Road. Records show that the second Eells house dates to 1888. After Eells passed away in 1903, that four-bedroom house has since been owned by H.H. Allyn, J.G. Bell (of Bonnie Bell Cosmetics), and Ed Meyers, among others. That 3,766 square foot edifice is still a distinctive private residence.

At 19581 Argyle Oval stands a house built in 2000, however for many years, there was a barn at that address, converted to a house, that dated back many decades. Residents are said to have included Mrs. Whiteside and George Kelly.

The land at Sunset Point was sold from the Eells estate to the Mathews & Gilbert real estate firm. K.D. Bishop constructed a distinctive white stucco mansion with a green tile roof and Italian Riviera architecture there in the early 1900s. He listed his street address as "Oakwood on the Lake, Rocky River, Ohio." Bishop was part of a company known as Bishop-Babcock-Becker that made soda fountains, novelty ice boxes, beer taps and hydraulic beer pumps using liquid carbonic gas. Their Cleveland operation was based at East 48th Street and Hamilton Avenue. (One of the company's antique World War I-era hand-pushed air pumps was recently listed on the International Military Antiques website for collectors for $99.) Bishop was also a life member of the New England Society of Cleveland, where fellow members included John D. Rockefeller, Charles Brush, Samuel Mather and other prominent industrialists.

At some point, the home became vacant and in 1928-1929, Frank Teshera proposed building a 178-suite luxury apartment complex to be called the Sunset Point Club. Neighbors objected and the City Council rejected the proposal. One can only imagine how different the community would be if apartments were constructed.

During the Depression, unpaid taxes on the property mounted. Lee Wilson, whose engineering business was headquartered on Lake Road in Rocky River opposite Cornwall Road, bought the mansion in a sheriff's sale in 1935 for the cost of the back taxes. Wilson, who was born in 1902, was another of the industrialists to make his home in Rocky River. His company became known for expertise in wire annealing furnaces and his team earned a number of patents. An active boater, Wilson was a past CYC commodore. An annual tradition was on Halloween night, as youngsters made their way door to door collecting candy in the Tangletown neighborhood, the folks at the mansion served hot apple cider, allowing the children to warm up a bit on those often-chilly evenings. His daughter, Nancylee Malm and her husband Dr. Lawrence

Malm, lived next door. The family owned the Sunset Point property until the mid-1980s.

Figure 31 - Sunset Point on the right during the Frank Mosier era. (Ken Winters, U.S. Army Corps of Engineers)

The mansion was later owned by BP America President Frank Mosier. During his time there, the abode was decorated with impressive oil paintings that complemented the home's design and stained-glass windows. In 2013, in an end of an era, the mansion was leveled. To maximize the property value, the land was split into several properties and new homes were built. One of those homes has been owned by Chris Antonetti, president of the Cleveland Indians/Guardians baseball team.

The beach area west of Sunset Point is known as Oakwood Beach. It is held in trust for the use and enjoyment of area residents. (In a different type of "use and enjoyment," during Prohibition, those smuggling bootleg liquor by boat sometimes placed their deliveries in a netted bag and attached them to the bottom of the pier; docked their boat without concern that agents would find the hooch; and then surreptitiously came around on foot or by car to retrieve their bottles.) Through the years, countless residents have enjoyed swimming, sunbathing, dog walks, fishing and cookouts at this convenient, private park. But the park also had a cautionary aspect to its history, which is addressed in the next chapter.

A Civic Response to Drownings

Oakwood Beach is a private park maintained for the enjoyment of residents of the Beach Cliff Number One neighborhood. It is on the shore of Lake Erie, just west of the Sunset Point cliff, and is located on land placed in reserve by Daniel Eells, the previous owner of Sunset Point.

The year was 1925 when a number of women living in the neighborhood went door to door to raise money to hire a lifeguard for Oakwood Beach. More than one swimmer had drowned and community leaders were alarmed. One of the perks of living in the neighborhood had become a threat to the survival of their sons and daughters. This led to the formation of the Women's Improvement Association of Oakwood and Beach Cliff Number One, which over time became known as the Beach Cliff Biddies. Through the years, the club raised money for the less fortunate, volunteered for the Red Cross, and sponsored swimming lessons. Many of the leading lady citizens of Rocky River have served as presidents of the organization, including this author's mother. The organization was still functioning nearly 100 years later. That civic spirit and determination to meet every challenge has long been part of what makes Rocky River a special community.

The Van Dorn Family

The United States began industrializing on a large scale in the 1870s. Greater Cleveland was well positioned to help lead this megatrend, given its proximity to natural resources, newly constructed rail lines, and the Great Lakes. Another man who capitalized on these opportunities also had strong Rocky River ties. His name was James Van Dorn. He grew up in Lorain, was trained as a blacksmith apprentice, and then worked for about nine years for a farm-machinery manufacturing firm in Akron. In the early 1870s, he established his own business in Akron, focusing on iron fencing.

Both ambitious and clever, Van Dorn met with city officials in Cleveland, Chicago and Cincinnati to discuss economic-development incentives to relocate his business. In this regard, he was decades ahead of his time. The City of Cleveland stepped up and provided a free, one-acre parcel of land on East 79th Street in the Kinsman neighborhood, near the Nickel Plate and the Pennsylvania railroad lines. Van Dorn seized the offer.

Over a period of more than 30 years, Van Dorn Iron Works became the leading supplier of wrought-iron fences and prisons, which Van Dorn said were little more than "fences built indoors." The company made the steel and iron framework for commercial buildings, the steel intake cribs for water plants, and the iron superstructure for the Detroit-Superior High-Level Bridge, which was built by Cleveland's King Bridge Company. In the early 1900s, Van Dorn was still innovating, introducing advances in mechanical dump-truck hoists. The company also manufactured security mailboxes, as well as steel furniture that was purchased by the U.S. Library of Congress.

James Van Dorn married, started a family, and made his primary home at 2697 Woodhill Road on Cleveland's east side. During this era, it was fashionable for the wealthy to build summer homes out in the country. Rockport (Rocky River) was still considered to be a peaceful, rural setting. Van Dorn built a stunning summer home in 1902 at 19420 Frazier Drive, not far from Daniel Eells' mansion. Van Dorn's home overlooked the river valley and the lake. As such, it was one of the grandest homes on Cleveland's west side.

By the 1910s, as the automobile made it easier to commute to Cleveland, some property owners began treating their summer homes in Rocky River as their year-around residence. James Van Dorn died suddenly of a heart attack in 1914 at age 73, but his son James Van Dorn, Jr. and grandson Thomas Van Dorn, lived in the beautiful Frazier Drive house. (A member of this same family owned an upscale women's clothing store in Rocky River in the 1980s on Detroit Road. Called Van Dorn & Company, the store offered women's business and fashion attire.) The Van Dorn Iron Works expanded into plastics and can manufacturing by the middle of the Twentieth Century. It closed its East 79th Street plant in 1991 and was bought out by Crown Cork and Seal in 1993.

By the 1960s, the home at 19420 Frazier was owned by the Ferry family, co-owners of the Ferry Cap and Screw industrial company. In 1992, the home caught on fire and sustained terrible damage. The evening fire was visible from the main dining room of the Cleveland Yachting Club, where members having dinner were shocked to see the landmark home ablaze.

Figure 32 - Following the 1992 fire at 19420 Frazier Drive (author's collection)

Figure 33 - House being completely rebuilt retaining only the historic facade (author's collection)

Happily, the home was rebuilt with the same architecture, restoring a familiar site to the riverfront. In 2020, the home was listed on Realtor.com at just under $2.8 million. A plaque in front of the abode celebrates the home's fascinating history.

A Brewing Magnate's Estate and Legacy

Schlather Lane today is a short residential street that runs through the former Rocky River estate of Leonard Schlather. This resourceful German immigrant operated a highly profitable brewery at the intersection of West 28th Street and Carroll Avenue in Cleveland. He owned the L. Schlather brewery from 1857 until 1902, when he sold it to the Cleveland & Sandusky Brewing Company for a large profit. Cleveland & Sandusky, in turn, was around until Prohibition.

Schlather's arrival in the United States makes for a good story. Leonard had two older brothers who made plans to travel by ship from Europe to the United States to seek their fortune. The young men's mother evidently became distraught over them moving so far from home, and one brother backed out. Since the ticket for the ship was already paid for, the story goes, 19-year-old Leonard hastily packed his bag and made the journey. He wound up achieving great success in the United States.

Leonard initially worked in a brewery in Altoona, Pennsylvania, where the family had relatives, before relocating to Cleveland. After working briefly for Hughes Brewery in the Flats, Schlather started his own operation. His success required the construction of a second brewery, and much of the wood used to build it is said to have come from the trees of his Rocky River landholding, which were cut, loaded onto wagons, and transported by horse-drawn wagon on the 1850 toll bridge over the Rocky River to his Cleveland construction site.

By the late 1870s, his brewing facility was arguably Cleveland's largest. He also owned an estimated 60 pubs, which was a terrific way to stoke demand for his tasty product. While building his business, Schlather found time to help raise seven daughters with his first wife, who passed away years before him.

The brewer lived across the street from his brewery on the near west side, where a Saint Ignatius athletic field is now located. The Rocky River property, at 2185 Wooster Road, was essentially a summer home. It was situated on more than 90 acres, stretching all the way to today's Public Library on the west, and overlooking the river valley on the east. The property even included a charming Japanese garden. Some of the land was used to grow hay, which Schlather had harvested and hauled downtown to feed the horses that pulled beer-delivery wagons.

Figure 34 - Leonard Schlather Painting (RR Public Library)

If you made a top ten list of the most influential couples in Rocky River history, Schlather and his second wife Sophia, 30 years his junior, would be on the list. After his retirement, they traveled the world, collecting fine paintings and books that are now exhibited in the Schlather Section of the Rocky River Public Library. Leonard passed away at his Cleveland residence in 1918, but Sophia continued to live in Rocky River for the rest of her life. She remained engaged in church and community affairs into her 90s. Sophia's $100,000 contribution in the 1950s funded the Public Library's first major expansion. Mrs. Schlather died on January 2, 1956 at the age of 91. Upon her death, her estate including the land was valued at just over $1.85 million, according to an Associated Press account. She divided her estate among family members, Case Institute of Technology, Baldwin-Wallace College, St. Luke's Hospital, the Cleveland Institute of Art, and other institutions. Today, the Cliff Towers Condominiums, at 2039-2089 Wooster Road, occupy much of the former Schlather estate. These five-floor condo buildings were constructed in 1963. The Great Lakes Brewing Company, established in 1988, now occupies buildings that were Schlather's Cleveland horse stables and barrel storage facility. A nearby plaque highlights this history.

A Well-Connected Attorney

Another longtime Rocky River resident from the 1930s to the 1970s is well worth remembering. Joseph Breitenstein was a Canton native who earned a law degree at Georgetown University in Washington, D.C. Breitenstein became the private secretary from 1911 to 1915 to U.S. Senator Atlee Pomerene, an Ohio Democrat. In those days, it was not uncommon for a senator's private secretary to wear numerous hats, including chief of staff, legislative director and press secretary.

Senator Pomerene's nickname was "the gloomy senator," but that was not an insult. It reflected Pomerene's sense of political courage, fairness and independence, and willingness to take unpopular stands. Those were unusual qualities in the world of politics even then. It spoke volumes about Joe Breitenstein's integrity that Pomerene would trust him as his confidential secretary.

By 1928, Breitenstein had an impressive resume of his own. Though he had lost his first bid for public office (a congressional race in 1918), he had served as assistant district attorney for the northern district of Ohio for seven years, handling important cases including *U.S. v. Eugene Debs*. He had also been secretary for the Ohio Democratic Party. That summer, the Democrats held their presidential nominating convention in Houston (a site selection made practical only by the recent development of air conditioning). Pomerene sought the Democratic presidential nomination as a favorite son candidate. Joe Breitenstein was there, making the speech that nominated Pomerene on the convention floor. Democrats ultimately tapped Al Smith of New York as their candidate and Smith went on to lose to Herbert Hoover that November.

Breitenstein had lived at the Cleveland Athletic Club at 1118 Euclid Avenue for a number of years, but finally settled down in 1931. He married a beautiful bride, Zita Clarke, from Sylvania, Ohio. The couple celebrated their wedding at the prestigious Mayflower Hotel in Washington, D.C., and in 1935 built a lovely home that is still standing at 265 Cornwall Road in Rocky River.

Figure 35 - The Breitenstein House at 265 Cornwall (courtesy of Zillow)

Once married, Joe Breitenstein made another run for Congress in 1934, seeking to dislodge fellow Democrat Martin L. Sweeney in the party primary. This was a high-profile race. Sweeney had gone to the 1932 Democratic convention supporting Al Smith but flipped his support to Franklin Roosevelt. Then in 1933, after losing a primary-election race for mayor of Cleveland, Sweeney backed the GOP candidate, Harry Davis. Many Democrats were livid and encouraged Breitenstein to try to topple Sweeney. Ultimately, Breitenstein's 1934 insurgent primary campaign was unsuccessful, but the next year, Ohio Governor Martin Davey appointed Breitenstein as special counsel for a public inquiry into fees paid to bank liquidators.

Breitenstein continued to practice law in downtown Cleveland all the way into the 1970s, even after suffering a stroke, when he was more than 80 years of age. His practice specialized in tax law, probate, and real estate, but he also was a close adviser to countless clients on a wide variety of legal, political, and business matters. His daily routine was to put on his suit and tie, walk to the bus stop on Beach Cliff Boulevard, ride downtown, and then make the return trip in the afternoon. His wife Zita was a real estate agent with Cleary Realty and was the agent who sold this author's family their home at 19986 Beach Cliff Boulevard in 1966. The couple is buried in Holy Cross Cemetery in Cleveland. In recent years, the house on Cornwall has been owned by Karl Kleinert, who grew up nearby on Beach Cliff Boulevard.

Streets with Recognized Names

How do streets get named? Most often the names are selected by land developers and approved by local governments. In Rocky River, streets are named after mayors, truck farmers, prominent business owners, developers and other leading citizens who helped make the city the quintessential suburb that it is today.

In the early part of the Twentieth Century, Rocky River was sometimes called the garden spot of Northeast Ohio. Farms and later greenhouses dominated the Rocky River landscape and also yielded the names of several city streets. One of the major greenhouse owners was Joseph M. Gasser, who arrived in 1883 and died in 1908. Gasser Boulevard, which runs north and south between Hilliard and Center Ridge on land he once owned, is named for him.

The Christensen family was active in greenhouse operations and civic affairs. Chrisfield Road, which is south of Center Ridge and developed in the 1970s, is named for the family; the nearby Marlys Drive is named for Marlys Christensen, who was Sunny's wife; and Sunnyhill Drive, which runs parallel with Center Ridge, is named for Sunny Christensen himself. Kramer Drive, a short street to the west of Lakeview Avenue, is named for the family that owned and operated Kramer's Flowers at 2054 Lakeview. Kramer Drive was developed in 1957.

Beach Cliff Boulevard is named after former Congressman and landowner Clifton Beach. His fascinating story was covered in a previous chapter.

Today's Wright Avenue, which was developed in the 1930s, is named for the Wright family. Rufus Wright spearheaded construction of the first bridge over the river, owned Wright's Tavern, and was a local postmaster. Wright Avenue begins at Detroit Road and runs southward to Dorothy Avenue. It is said that the street did not extend past Dorothy Avenue because a local farmer would not sell a right of way. Dorothy Avenue is named for Dorothy Simonds, a descendant of Rufus Wright. She was born in 1889.

Allen Court, a short north-south street off of Detroit near the Rocky River United Methodist Church, was named by landowner Philotas McMahon after his wife Mary Allen. She traced her family lineage to Revolutionary War patriot Ethan Allen. Members of the Bowles family indicate that when the original Silverthorn Inn was torn down, they reused some of the beams in the construction of a small white house with green awnings, shown below, at 1223 Allen Court. Real estate records show that the house was built in 1919, which adds credence to the story. For many years the edifice was home to the Zbin family, which runs a landscaping business at 1209 Linda Street.

The home on Allen Court was later owned by the Spremulli family, operators of the nearby service station, for investment and rental purposes. The Spremulli's sold this and several other Allen Court properties in 2025 to GKHE Properties. The "White Cottage" at 1338 Allen Court dates to 1900, according to public records, and has been the home to retail businesses. The nearby Parsons Court was developed in the 1890s and memorializes a developer named Parsons.

Figure 36 - Century home at 1223 Allen Court dating to 1919 (courtesy of Zillow)

Ingersoll Drive is the short east-west street that connects Smith Court with Linda Street. The Lake Shore Electric (or Interurban) streetcar used to travel down Linda Street, turn on the right-of-way (today's Ingersoll Drive), and then make another right on Smith Court. The Ingersoll family owned the land on both sides of the right-of-way, so when the streetcar ceased operations in 1938, it seemed to make sense for the family to buy the right-of-way. Eventually, they handed the street over to the City for purposes of services such as snow plowing. By the 1970s, Ingersoll Drive had become an eyesore, little more than a street-long junkyard. Over time, the City and private landowners saw to it that it was cleaned up and redeveloped. This is yet another example of the spirit of problem-solving emblematic of Rocky River and its residents. These days, the street is home to businesses like Paragon Health and Fitness, Earnest Machine Products, and an office building.

Linda Street has enjoyed a revitalization in recent years as several former residences have been converted into thriving businesses. The street also includes several older buildings. The small structure at 539 Linda Street, shown below, was built in 1884, back when Chester Arthur was the President of the United States.

Figure 37 - The 141-year-old home at 539 Linda Street (author's collection)

Macbeth Drive, which runs southeast off of Wooster Road and overlooks the valley, is named for the Macbeth family, which owned property south of the Schlather land holdings. Thomas Macbeth owned the Bruce Macbeth Engine Company at 2111 Center Street in Cleveland. (That industrial building now has historic status, having housed the Eclipse Iron Works foundry, then Macbeth's business, followed by Tenk Machine & Tool Company. Now it's an event center that hosted high-profile receptions during the 2016 Republican National Convention.)

Thomas Macbeth married an immigrant from Wales named Emily, and the couple raised four children. The Welsh Home, Rocky River Public Library, and Rocky River United Methodist Church all reflect major financial contributions from the Macbeths. Thomas Macbeth passed away in 1938 and the family home was knocked down in 1940. Donald Macbeth – Thomas and Emily's son – developed Macbeth Drive as a private street, with no city services or sidewalks, mostly in the 1950s. A couple of homes used by Donald Macbeth and his sister, Catherine Macbeth Hubbard, date back further.

South of Macbeth Drive just north of Interstate 90 is Mitchell Avenue, which was developed between 1915 and 1920. This older street is named for Mark Mitchell, who was the first mayor of the Village of Rocky River, as well as a land developer. It was originally a dirt road. Today, there are only houses on the north side, but until the Interstate was built, there were also homes on the south side. Also nearby is Morley Avenue (formerly Morley Court), developed around the same time, which is named for Fred and Gertrude Morley, who ran the old general store at the corner of Center Ridge Road and Wooster Road. The small city-owned Morley Park is at the end of the street.

The land on which Morley Park is located was donated to the city by John Struhar. After working as a carpenter early in his career, he became a developer and home builder in several of the western suburbs in the 1950s. Struhar Drive, which runs parallel to Wooster Road, is named for him. Struhar also named Sheron Drive after his grandchildren Sherry and Ron. This street was demolished in the late 1960s in preparation for the Route 90 construction project.

Colahan Drive, which intersects with Wooster Road, is parallel to Mitchell Avenue. It was named for Solon Colahan, the truck farmer who owned land in that area. The street was developed in the 1958 to 1960 period. Solon Colahan was the father of Harry Colahan, and grandfather of Harris Colahan, who were associated with the appliance store that carried their family name in downtown Rocky River.

Wooster Road was initially called Mastick Road, named for the family of Benjamin Mastick. Originally from Vermont, Mastick moved to Rockport Township and began serving on the township board of trustees off and on starting in 1848. He fathered nine children, and upon his death in 1872, he was buried in Fairview Park Cemetery, which is located at West 196th Street and Lorain Road.

Gibson Drive, south of Hilliard Boulevard in the western part of the city, is named for Frank Gibson, the mayor during the early 1950s. The street was built out in the late 1950s.

The Story family members were early, rural landowners south of Center Ridge Road near Wooster Road. They had a small, private road running through their property, which eventually became Story Road, running all the way to Lorain Road. Today, Story Road is the fastest way to get from Rocky River to Cleveland Clinic Fairview Hospital and other points southeast. Homes on Story Road were constructed in the Forties, Fifties and Sixties.

Further west, John Spencer was a farmer and brick producer whose family owned land in southern Rocky River for decades. He was on the township board of trustees as early as 1843. Spencer Road, which runs southward from Center Ridge Road into Fairview

Park where it becomes West 220th Street, is named for this family, as is Spencer Creek, which flows through Elmwood Park and into both the Rocky River and Lake Erie.

Parallel to Spencer Road is Higley Road, named for Isaac Higley, whose family had owned land in Rockport since the 1860s. The property included the Higley's farmhouse and the same pond that is on the property today. In the winter, the pond would freeze and children would skate on it. According to Sunny Christensen, Higley would open a window in his home and play music for the children to enjoy while skating. In 1921, Higley sold his farmhouse, pond, and seven acres to the Welsh Home retirement center. The Welsh Home originally opened in 1911 in Cleveland Heights to provide a haven for aging individuals of Welsh heritage. Prominent socialites Emily Macbeth and Sophia Schlather were instrumental in getting the institution moved to Rocky River, and initially 29 residents lived in the large Higley farmhouse. The current facility was built in 1963, replacing the old farmhouse which was razed.

Palmer Drive, a short north-south street south of Center Ridge Road, was developed in the early 1970s. Sunny Christensen wrote that when John Struhar was developing the upscale West River Estates community, he needed some land owned by Palmer Meyers, Jr., who worked for the City service department. When the negotiations bogged down, Struhar sweetened his offer to name the street "Palmer" in honor of Palmer Meyers and his father. The tactic must have worked because the deal went through. Parallel to Palmer Drive and Higley Road is Thomson Circle. This street is named for another local family that operated a dry goods store in downtown Rocky River and a greenhouse. By the time the street was developed, five generations of Thomsons had lived in the city.

Bates Road, which starts at Detroit Road near Rocky River Presbyterian Church and runs north, was developed shortly after World War Two. It is named after Jonathan Bates, a truck farmer who owned and worked the land there. He was married to Hannah Saunderson Bates and their former home was right next to Bates Pond. Once the family leveled the home in 1962, Bates Pond became a favorite locale for local children to do some fishing. The pond is south of the Rocky River service garage. Bates School was named for this family, as well.

Wagar Road memorializes the family of Mars Wagar, who was originally from Saratoga, New York. He bought 111 acres of land in the future Lakewood, Ohio, in 1820. Some sources say he purchased the land from the Connecticut Land Company, making him one of the original landowners in the Western Reserve; other sources say he bought it from Francis Granger, son of Gideon Granger, who had hoped the entire region would be remembered as Granger City.

In either case, Mars Wagar was a surveyor and educator by trade and married a lady whose family lineage traced to John Alden, a crew member on the Mayflower. One acre of his land holdings was set aside for a cemetery and Wagar called it, "God's Acre." Eventually, as that section of Lakewood became an urban area, the graves were excavated and moved to Lakewood Park Cemetery in Rocky River. Mars Wagar's grave is next to the mass grave of persons who had been buried in God's Acre. He passed away in 1841 at age 50. The Wagar Beach park at the lakeshore, held in trust for residents of the Beach Cliff Number Two neighborhood at the end of the red-brick road, is named after the same family. During summers, lifeguards are on duty at Wagar Beach to ensure the safety of swimmers. The photo below shows Roxy, the dog of former Rocky Riverite Matt Groner, at the entrance to Wagar Beach in 2024.

Figure 38 - Matthew Groner's dog, Roxy, strikes a pose at the entrance to Wagar Beach. (Matthew Groner)

During the 1970s, on a day when the Rolling Stones were in Cleveland to perform a rock concert at Municipal Stadium, a Wagar Beach lifeguard returned from work that day telling family and friends that members of the band had shown up at the park that afternoon for a quick swim. Although the lifeguard may have fabricated the story, it nonetheless made for some interesting neighborhood conversation that summer.

In our hurried, modern-day life, many of us are too busy to even contemplate why streets received their names, and who was responsible for naming them. Especially in Rocky River, the street names are a history lesson unto themselves. For a list of nearly every Rocky River street and the year it was developed, see Appendix A.

Building Schools during the Baby Boom

Quality schools have been a hallmark of Rocky River for decades and the district is constantly ranked among the finest in Ohio by the state government and the local media. The school system has six strategic objectives, which include ensuring that students learn in state-of-the-art facilities and in an environment that is technologically competitive on a global level. A tremendous school system is an integral part of Rocky River's status as a quintessential suburb. When a Rocky River High School junior or senior applies for admission to a midwestern college or university, the institutions' admissions counselors often know of the high school's reputation for quality academics. This chapter examines the history of the schools, including the need for additional facilities during the 1950s and 1960s.

One of the foremost trends after the conclusion of World War II was the Baby Boom, which demographers define as starting in 1945 or 1946, and continuing through 1960 or 1964. With the war behind them, returning soldiers and factory workers alike were able to pursue their personal version of the American dream, which often included moving to the suburbs and starting families. Rocky River was no exception to the national trend. The largest population ever recorded by the Census Bureau was 22,958 in 1970, which was 25 years into the Baby Boom. By contrast, the earlier resident count at the end of the war was estimated at 10,000 or less.

The Rocky River School Board responded to population growth with decisive actions. One step was the construction of Rocky River High School at the corner of Detroit Road and Wagar Road. The two-level school, which included ample classrooms, two gymnasiums, a music room, and a swimming pool, opened in 1950. The land also included baseball fields and basketball courts. That investment allowed the older school building on Lakeview Avenue to be dedicated strictly to junior high school students.

Second, Goldwood School reopened as home building in southern Rocky River picked up. The building, which had been shuttered since the early 1930s, was upgraded and modernized, and some excellent baseball fields with dugouts and seating for family members, were built north of the school for use by students and the Rocky River Little League, which was established in 1952.

Third, the school system added a fifth elementary school to supplement Beach, Wooster, Kensington and Goldwood schools. Bates School opened to serve students in the west-central area of Rocky River, south of the railroad tracks. Bates was a more modern school in some ways, but had some odd features as well. On one side of the gymnasium, rather than a flat floor, there were wood steps leading to a slightly elevated platform or stage. The steps would represent a hazard for any student who was running in the gym – perhaps chasing down a loose ball on the basketball court – and not staying alert. In a fourth step related to the population boom, a "new" Wooster School opened in 1955, next to the existing building, which was renamed Wooster Annex.

Residents of Rocky River have consistently recognized the importance of education. Their commitment to quality schools is reflected in the school construction in the 20th Century and the passage of many school levies through the years.

During their heyday, there were enough students – and funds – to support five elementary schools, the junior high, and the high school. One of the great traditions was the autumn carnival held at a number of the schools. Young students could visit booths and play games of skill or chance. Prizes ranged from a few pennies to bubble gum to small toys to live turtles and goldfish. Below, students Liz Fahnert and Mark Krein pose with their moms Jean Fahnert and Evelyn Krein in a 1970 promotional photo for the Kensington Karnival. Both Liz and Mark went on to graduate from RRHS in 1978.

Figure 39 - 1970 Kensington Karnival promo photo (author's collection)

Other traditions included the dramatic performances and music concerts presented by the high school students as well as art exhibits at the elementary school level. At the

Junior High and later the high school, the excellent history teacher Harlan Radford staffed the Stamp Club and the Aviation Club, which toured the airport air traffic control center and other locales. Field trips for elementary school children included visiting a farm, the Warther Museum, Dover Dam, and Schoenbrun Village. High school students were taken to visit museums including the Salvador Dali museum which eventually relocated to Florida.

The Baby Boom was, of course, not a permanent trend, and the school district eventually retrenched from seven to just four schools – the High School, Junior High, Kensington Intermediate, and Goldwood Elementary. Of the five modern elementary schools, Bates had the shortest span of service, closing not long after the number of district students began to sharply decline.

This book would not be complete without some brief notes about schools from earlier eras. Several tiny schools evidently operated in the nineteenth century. The first in Rockport Township may have been operated ever so briefly in the early 1820s by Jonathan Parshall, who purchased some land from Mars Wagar in today's Lakewood. According to the *History of Cuyahoga County,* "Parshall was a house carpenter, and also taught school for a few weeks in Rockport, but he was not very industrious, and in the course of time, being unable to pay for even his half acre of land, he was disposed of it."

An 1874 map shows a school on Center Ridge Road. By the 1890s, there were a couple of schools operating. One was on Wooster Road near Center Ridge Road. It was originally focused on the lower grades and later added high-school curriculum. Another operated for a time on Detroit Road near Elmwood Road and was called the Dean school because it was built on land owned by the Dean family.

Beach Elementary School opened in 1897 on wooded land donated by Congressman Clifton Beach. Various challenges were encountered in those early years. Initially, there were only four classrooms, and crowding became a problem. There was no lighting, so evening activities were not practical. Classes were postponed for six weeks in 1918 due to the flu pandemic, a crisis with which modern readers can identify. A new Beach School building went into operation in 1930. Another challenge came in May 1956 when a windstorm caused the building's tall chimney to collapse onto the center of the edifice, crashing through to the basement floor. Thankfully, this happened on a weekend when the building was unoccupied. Repairs were quickly made and the school was as good as new again. Beach School remained in service until the 1981-1982 school year, when it was converted to an administrative building. The school system offices were moved there in 2013 and more recently, a pre-school moved into the building, too.

Wooster School opened in 1902, with major expansions in 1922 and 1945. The "new" Wooster School commenced classes in 1955 adjacent to the original building. That older building, as previously noted, was then called Wooster Annex and used for administrative purposes. Surprisingly, given its historic status, it was razed in 1991 and a plaque marks the site. When the district decided to operate only four schools, the newer Wooster School became expendable. It was torn down in 2013.

As the Beach Cliff Number One and Number Two neighborhoods were built out, it was a logical decision to provide these new communities with their own school. Kensington Elementary was built on Lake Road in 1927. The building originally had a main entrance on Lake Road, from which an auditorium was on the left, a small library and teacher offices were on the right, and the principal's office was straight ahead. A lower level included the boiler room as well as a gymnasium. The gym ceiling was extremely low, and any basketball shot with too high of an arc would hit the ceiling and be redirected. Given this problem, it was not surprising that students learning the fundamentals of basketball came away from Kensington shooting line-drive jump shots, rather than rainbow jumpers. Also on that level was a small room where the custodial staff – often joined by gym teacher Cliff Gallo – relaxed, drank coffee, and smoked cigarettes or pipes. Wings were added on the east and west sides of the building and a new gymnasium (with plenty of height) was finally added on the north side in the late 1970s.

The school system had planned in the 1920s to build a school at the corner of Northview Road and Center Ridge and purchased farmland from the Zeager family for that purpose. Once Goldwood School was built, the school board concluded it would not need the old Zeager land and it was sold. (The Zeager family's home was at 3644 Wooster Road. The old Zeager lot was redeveloped with several new homes a number of years ago.)

Goldwood School, the fourth of the elementary schools, was completed in 1928, having been built as an incentive for residents of Goldwood Township (which had been a separate jurisdiction since 1910) to align with Rocky River. It was named for Deborah Goldwood, the wife of local businessman and landowner John Spencer. But with the onset of the Depression, the anticipated enrollment at Goldwood failed to materialize. Hence, the school closed in 1931 and students were transferred to Beach School. The building sat empty until the Baby Boom kicked in.

Rocky River also has some private schools. The Ruffing Montessori School is located at 1285 Orchard Park Drive, in the former Bates School building. Magnificat is an all-girls high school on Hilliard Boulevard that opened in 1955. It has about 700 students. St. Christopher's School provides Catholic education for students through the eighth grade. Lutheran West is a co-ed high school at 3850 Linden Road that opened in 1958. In the mid-1950s, there was only one Lutheran high school in the region, located downtown. When that school was designated for demolition by the government as part of the construction of the Inner Belt highway, the Lutheran community decided to build two new schools – an eastern school in Cleveland Heights and a western school in Rocky River.

Further information about the high quality of public education in Rocky River is included in the chapter entitled, "The Promising Future."

The Greenhouse Capital of the Nation

Cuyahoga County was considered the greenhouse capital of the nation in the early decades of the 20th Century with 450 acres under glass! Rocky River hosted the County's largest concentration of these glass-covered agricultural facilities.

"The first greenhouse in Rocky River was the Gasser flower greenhouse, on the west side of Wooster Road, between Hilliard and Center Ridge roads," notes Gay Christensen-Dean. "They grew roses and other flowers." Joseph M. Gasser arrived in 1883 and owned 67 acres. Gasser, who had an attractive three-story home on Wooster, raised flowers year-around (in 15 acres of greenhouses) and shipped them to several states. After his 1908 death, family members kept the business afloat until 1927. Other flower-growing greenhouses were operated by the Kaiser, Snyder, Thompson and Kramer families. Kramer's Flowers was in business for many years at 2054 Lakeview.

The Christensen family was prominent in vegetable-growing greenhouses. According to Ms. Christensen-Dean, Charles Christian Christensen was born in Denmark in 1848 and served in the U.S. Navy before settling in Rocky River in 1881. "He bought a farm on the northwest corner of Wooster and Hilliard Roads, extending westerly to Lakeview Drive. It is exactly where Interstate 90 runs today," she adds. C.C.'s first greenhouse investment did so well that he quickly expanded the business. Money earned was redirected to buying more land. He and his wife had seven children, three of whom went into greenhouse ownership.

One of Charles' sons, George Christensen (Gay's grandfather), said that at his peak, he was averaging 50 tons of tomatoes per acre per year out of his 2.5 acre greenhouse. George married Laura Primett, whose father Archer Primett built the Primett building on Detroit Road. A second son, Carl, owned a greenhouse south of Center Ridge Road, where the Westwood Town Shopping Center (home to Marc's and Home Depot) is today. Carl's greenhouse opened in about 1910 and expanded to 3.5 acres under glass. Carl's son, Charles R. Christensen, ran the operation until selling the land in 1976. *WESTLIFE* covered the closure with a front-page story proclaiming the end of an era. A third son, Herman, ran a greenhouse business growing tomatoes and mushrooms on the southeast corner of Linden and Center Ridge Roads, where a bank is now located. Herman resided on Wooster Road until he passed away in 1958.

According to Gay, in 1909, the Christensen, Hoag, Petersen, Wind, Asplin, Pease and other families banded together to form the Rocky River Greenhouse Company, with a 3.75 acre greenhouse on the west side of Wooster Road, north of Story Road. Disagreements led to the Christensens and the Zeagers (their cousins) buying out the other parties. This operation lasted until about 1964. Following the split-up, the Hoag family independently operated a greenhouse south of Center Ridge Road.

Meanwhile, George's son Sunny Christensen (Gay's father), bought a greenhouse at 22487 Center Ridge Road, where the upscale West River Estates homes are now located. Sunny, a third-generation resident, closed his business in July 1962. He had earned a law degree and served on the City Council, before passing away in 1998. His extensive notes were later compiled by Gay to become the book *Incidents and Episodes,* which gives a first-hand flavor for local history. In a presentation to the Rocky River Historical Society on May 8, 2003, Gay noted that her mother Marlys Christensen was the first national president of the women's auxiliary to the Vegetable Growers Association of America, and Arline Christensen succeeded her.

Greenhouses have always been energy-intensive operations. In the early years, Rocky River's operators used coal to heat their facilities. Later, some relied on natural gas, and the suburb's landscape was marked by natural gas towers. By the 1960s, the business was becoming less economical for several reasons. First, energy costs continued to rise. Second, refrigerated rail cars and trucks meant that flowers and vegetables grown far away now were competitive with locally grown products. Third, Mexico was becoming a source of competition. Fourth and finally, land values in Rocky River were rising as the city was becoming the quintessential suburb that it is today. Accordingly, the greenhouse owners had no trouble selling their land to commercial and residential property developers.

A 2022 report suggested that there are about 8,700 greenhouse farms remaining in the United States. Pennsylvania, New York and California are now said to be the leading greenhouse states. Local residents wishing to visit greenhouses now travel to Westlake and North Ridgeville.

In a nod to Rocky River's history and future, Magnificat High School is planning to build a 1,873 square foot greenhouse within its garden as an educational resource. Please see Appendix C for a list of Rocky River greenhouses circa 1927.

The Third Wave of Memorable Businesses (1900 to 1950)

At the turn of the century, the leaders of Rockport Township were looking enthusiastically to the future. Having become an independent hamlet in 1891, local leaders sought the advantages that would come with being designated by the state as the village of Rocky River, and officially achieved that status in 1903, the same year that Ohio celebrated its centennial.

Rocky River at the turn of the century had perhaps 500 residents and was still a largely rural community. Undeveloped areas were still mostly forested. Many acres were increasingly dedicated to farming, greenhouses and truck gardens (as noted in the previous chapter). Truck gardens were small, family-owned farms that produced vegetables, fruit or flowers and delivered products directly to retailers, absent any distributor.

In addition to agriculture, Rocky River still hosted tourists who were passing through or who sought an escape from Cleveland for a few days. Tourism was lively during the summer and also somewhat active during the other seasons. As Sunny Christensen said, the Cuyahoga River was the industrial river and the Rocky River was the recreational river.

One example of tourism was Hahn's Grove. The area was initially called McMahon's Run (named for an owner of the beachfront property who arrived in 1831). The Charles Hahn family bought 10 acres and built about 20 beachfront cabins, which were leased out to vacationers. In all likelihood, few of the renters contemplated being on the site of Bradstreet's Disaster. The presence of Hahn's Grove is the likely reason that the Interurban services stopped there. The Hahns sold the property in 1946. (The Beach Cliff Place Apartments were built on the southern side of the property in 1963, and the Beach House condominium was built on the north side in 1975.)

The City's population began to grow in the 1920s and 1930s, then accelerated sharply following the conclusion of World War II. Land was gradually prepared for housing subdivisions, a country club, a cemetery, and retail. Signs of growth were evident in 1923 as the City adopted its first parking regulations, purchased land for a water disposal plant, and convinced the County to extend and improve Hilliard Boulevard. The fire department was organized a year later.

To serve the growing population, more businesses opened, each one contributing to the social fabric of the community. Initially, these were mostly family-owned businesses; but by 1950, a growing number of chain stores had planted roots in the suburb.

The Rocky River Chamber of Commerce was established "to protect the moral, social, business, and civic interests" of Rocky River. The year it was founded was 1922, according to the Chamber website, or 1938, according to a book by the Historical Society. In the years since, the Chamber has provided a structure in which business leaders can interact with one another, government leaders, and the public to foster economic growth, job creation and a high standard of living.

The largest concentration of businesses in 1900 was still downtown, over the bridge from Lakewood. One of the movers and shakers was Archer John Primett. A trained butcher, he operated his Oakwood Market on Detroit Road across from the Silverthorn, and later on Old Lake Road (then Blount Street), offering the best cuts of meat, chicken and fish he could procure, as well as vegetables grown on his own farm. Consumers lacked refrigeration solutions so most went to the market daily. In 1909 he built the Primett Building (still in use), the City's first masonry structure. His meat market was on the first level and he resided in the apartment above it. He rented out the store and apartment on the other side. The Primett building later became the City Hall, with the city jail on the lower level and the fire department with several garage bays at the rear. For a time, the second floor served as the high school. It made for an interesting dynamic for school kids to hear fire department sirens and pass by prisoners.

Archer Primett also served on the hamlet council and developed Rockland Avenue, a north-south street that runs from Detroit Road eight blocks to Purnell Avenue. Primett married Anna Saunderson, whose foster parents were truck gardeners Jonathan and Hannah Saunderson Bates. The Primetts were related by marriage to the Christensen family that was active in the greenhouse industry and civic affairs. Primett and his wife moved west to Sheffield Lake in 1924, selling their Rocky River business to Charlie Thomson. The Primett Building has stood the test of time and is still serving the downtown community.

Figure 40 - The Primett Building, Rocky River's first brick structure (author's collection)

At one point, Bash's dry-goods store was right next door. Mark Mitchell, an immigrant from Great Britain who was Rocky River's first village mayor from 1903 to 1913, ran his blacksmith shop nearby. William Hoag – another pivotal figure – operated a feed, grain, tile, cement and coal store that served all of the agricultural and construction interests in the area. The coal, delivered by railroad, was needed to power the greenhouses until natural gas became a more viable option. A small, two-room post office was attached to the side of Hoag's store from 1910 to 1938. The postmaster position in those days was a political patronage job. Whenever a new party won control of the White House, Rocky River got a new postmaster. The small post office building was torn down around 1940.

Nearby on today's Lake Road, across the street from the Hotel Westlake in the 1920s and/or 1930s, was a barber shop operated by John Gall (or Gaul), Boor's Drugstore, and the First National Bank of Rocky River. The bank was chartered in 1923, with Frank Mitchell (the Rocky River city clerk) and John Hoag as the proprietors. Future mayor Carl Stein was a vice president at the bank. In the classic postcard below which looks North toward the lake, notice the railroad trestle on the far right that still stands today. The Silverthorn Tavern and its white fence are discernible on the lower right corner. The businesses on the left include John Gall's Barber Shop, Boor's Drugstore, the First National Bank of Rocky River, Schwartz's Bicycle Shop and Ingersoll's Hardware on the corner of North Ridge, or Old Detroit Road.

Figure 41 - Classic postcard showing downtown more than 100 years ago. (Courtesy of Harlan Radford)

Achieving a federal bank charter was no small doing in that era, but John Hoag and other local leaders pulled together the funding and paperwork to make it happen. Their motivation was to have locally managed banking that would serve the needs of the community. Too often, they believed, the big banks in Cleveland were taking advantage of small suburban businesses. And when the Guardian Trust Bank went under during the Depression, the thriving First National Bank of Rocky River moved into the Guardian Bank's more attractive office. This influential bank was purchased in 1945 by National City Bank, and John Hoag stayed until he retired in 1949. Hoag, who also operated greenhouses and a basket factory, resided at 22830 Detroit Road (a newer home was built on that lot in 1973, just east of the Crown Water Filtration Plant). Hoag and his wife Edna played such an integral role in the fabric of Rocky River life that a memorial garden and marker near Rocky River City Hall honor their memory.

National City was intent on making sure that people knew it had arrived. The bank posted its name in large block lettering from the building's roof, which was visible from the Rocky River bridge all the way through the end of the 1970s. Driving in from Lakewood, the bank's signage was one of the first things anyone would see.

Schwartz's Bakery made deliveries using an early Ford truck. The Sprague Grocery Store was across the street from the Silverthorn. Ingersoll's Hardware previously was

The Third Wave of Memorable Businesses (1900 to 1950)

a dry goods store operated by Geiger & Keyse. William J. Geiger, originally from Dover (Bay Village), resided at 1724 Wooster Road for 51 years. He first opened the hardware store in 1890 before selling it to Frank Ingersoll in 1908. Geiger later focused on banking and real-estate development. Those looking for some libation or a meal had several choices early in the new Century. William (Billy) White ran White's Saloon in a three-story wood building on Lake Road and Kennedy's Saloon was just steps away, as was the Silverthorn, which was purchased by the Morton family in 1900. The original Silverthorn operated until 1917, when the Mortons moved to Lakewood and sold the 107-year-old building to the Fowler-Welman-Kelly Company for redevelopment.

The elegant Hotel Westlake arrived in the 1920s on the old Silverthorn lot and Rocky River's streetscape changed dramatically. Tourism had traditionally centered around picnics, boat rentals, and frolicking in the clean waters of the Rocky River or Lake Erie. Now, well-dressed aviators, flight attendants, and traveling sales executives began arriving for short-term stays in this new luxury hotel that became a local landmark (as explored in another chapter). During the World War I years, in the riverfront area that would soon become the Hotel Westlake's backyard, the Rocky River Dry Dock Company was in operation (see the earlier chapter about the military in Rocky River).

One of Rocky River's most popular stores, the Original Candyland, began as a vending stand operated by Peter and Steve Sougianis in 1910 on land leased from the Silverthorn. After the business moved across the street to 19015 Lake Road in about 1923 and became known as Candyland, customers entered an impressive store with deluxe tile flooring, decorative ceilings, and a then-rare-mechanized soda fountain, which took advantage of modern advances in refrigeration. Brother-in-law George Souris's name was on the original 1918 lease, but the family is unaware of any other role that Souris had with Candyland. George's wife, Sirmalenia, the sister of Peter and Steve, operated The Elite, a lunch counter restaurant, directly north of and adjacent to Candyland, according to Bill Osgood. Candyland patrons enjoyed hand-dipped candies, soft drinks and a choice of fine cigars. Going to Candyland was one of the joys of life, whether for family outings, young couples on a date, or for guests at the Westlake. Always a family-owned business, one of the family members lived in an apartment above the store, while Steve Sougianis's family resided not far away in a home at 1656 Wooster Road that dated back to before 1900, according to Osgood.

Figure 42 - Candyland has brought joy to many hundreds of customers. (Permission of Bill Osgood and The Original Candyland)

As shown in the photograph, customers could view products in the display cases and enjoy their refreshments or treats in the seating area. Following a death in the family, the retail location closed in 1952. Around 1962, the family re-entered the candy business, operating out of their home on Wooster Road. In 1968, to accommodate the growing popularity of Candyland, additional manufacturing and retail space was added, along with a new entrance.

(Today, the business is operated by Mr. and Ms. Bill Osgood. Bill is a 1967 RRHS graduate and the grandson of Steve Sougianis. A broad variety of chocolate candies can be ordered from TheOriginalCandyland.com or by visiting the business at 2235 East Enterprise Parkway in Twinsburg on Tuesdays through Sundays except for certain holidays and summer months. The phone number is 330-405-1994. Tommy's restaurant and bar was later located in this building before relocating to Linda Street. The popular seafood restaurant Salmon Dave's has occupied this historic space since 1993.)

Early in the century, a livery stable for the tending of horses was maintained by the Demaline family across the street from the Primett meat market. The Beach-Colahan store came later and was located in the bank complex. It offered a selection of radios, car tires, and for a number of years had a gasoline hand pump out front. A physician, Dr. Hastings, had his home and medical office in this neighborhood. Also downtown was the Spitzig Bank, next to Ingersoll's Hardware. On the other side of the railroad tracks, near where Yacht Club Drive connects with Beach Cliff Boulevard, was the Freeland realty agency. Further west on Detroit opposite of Lakeview Avenue was the Jordan Lumber Company. Their lot ran all the way north to the railroad tracks, so it's probable that there was a rail spur in place for lumber deliveries. There was also a football field on their premises used by the Rocky River schools. This business was located where today's Rocky River Adult Activity Center is situated. Sorenson's Grocery operated at the corner of Detroit Road and Northview Road, not far from the current Martin's Corner food store. Further west on the other side of Wagar Road was the Bates family truck-garden operation.

There was a basket factory at 19537 Lake Road behind the Barrett Creamery. While that doesn't sound like a lucrative enterprise today, in the early Twentieth Century there was ample money to be made by selling baskets to greenhouse owners and truck-garden operators. John Hoag had a business interest in this company, and his in-law, Sion Wenban, was the factory's manager. Much as he did with the local bank, Hoag established the business in large part because Cleveland-based basket suppliers were charging suburban greenhouses and truck farmers exorbitant prices. Hoag remedied the problem by starting his own business. The basket factory sustained a fire in 1941, but it was ultimately the drop-off in the truck-farming and greenhouse industries that spelled the enterprise's end. A 1920 commercial building occupied by Lakeside Produce Distribution is now at that site, as are the Inner Bliss Yoga Studio and several other small businesses.

Hoag's Lake Road operation was not the only local basket company. In the early 1900s, the Asplin family manufactured baskets near a pond in the Spencer Road area in southern Rocky River. Henry Asplin's son, Howard, operated a greenhouse north of Center Ridge Road, and was naturally one of his dad's customers.

The Forest City Ice Company operated from a very large building alongside the river at today's Clifton Beach in Lakewood. The ice was harvested from the frozen lake during the winter by men with chainsaws. If excess snow was covering the ice, horse-drawn plows cleared the snow. It is remarkable to contemplate how thick the ice had to have been to support the weight of men, horses and plows. Once the ice was cut into blocks, it was floated down a man-made channel to the building at Clifton Beach, where it was stored between layers of sawdust, which prevented the blocks from melting together. This is a classic example of a business that became obsolete due to technology – in this case the advent of modern refrigeration and freezers.

In the 1940s, the corner of Detroit Road and West 192nd Street featured the Rocky River Hardware Store, a competitor to Ingersoll's. The side of this store had a painted advertisement for Lowe Brothers Paint (a Dayton-based paint brand that was later bought out by Sherwin-Williams). Next door was a jewelry store with a large vertical sign touting Elgin watches. Based in Elgin, Illinois (west of Chicago), Elgin was a major maker of watches until the company folded in 1968. A food store was next door to the jewelry shop. Ingersoll's, of course, was across the street, with an advertisement for Glidden Paint tinted onto its side wall.

The Duet Building on Wooster Road between Riverwood and Shoreland was constructed in the 1920s. Many businesses operated there, including the Riverwood Drugstore in the 1940s.

These and other business enterprises from 1900 to 1950 met residents' daily needs and contributed to the development of Rocky River. Memorable businesses from 1950 to present are highlighted in a later chapter. Let's turn next to the fascinating story of one of Rocky River's most recognizable landmarks, the Hotel Westlake.

The Hotel Westlake's Storied History

The third decade of the Twentieth Century is remembered as the "Roaring Twenties." They certainly roared at the Hotel Westlake. Built in 1923 by the Miramar Apartments Company, the property enjoyed roughly the same strategic location overlooking the river as its predecessors, Wright's Tavern and the Silverthorn Inn, the latter of which was torn down several years earlier. From the day it opened, the "Pink Palace" offered the high life to those who sought a luxury lifestyle and had the resources to pay for it.

Figure 43 - Postcard view of the back of the Hotel Westlake (author's collection)

With a distinctive stucco exterior and large "Hotel Westlake" signage on the roof, the new property became a defining landmark. The lavish interior offered a lobby with comfortable seating and writing desks, along with a mezzanine level where cigar-smoking men congregated, and where the Marine Dining Room offered stunning river views. Long-term suites and short-term room rentals were available. There was also the Commodore Lounge, smaller rooms for card games, a barber shop, a beauty shop, and a lower-level dry cleaner.

A glossy weekly magazine kept residents abreast of local news and upcoming events in Cleveland. Behind the property – where just a few years earlier had been a drydock facility – was a marina, miniature golf, tennis court, children's playground, horse stables, and lush, well-maintained gardens. Private golf lessons were offered onsite. The riverfront location also was convenient for the occasional rumrunner surreptitiously delivering supplies during Prohibition.

As noted in the book *Rocky River Yesterday*, "The historical significance of The Westlake Hotel to our community lies not in dates and facts surrounding the building, but in the hearts of tens of thousands of guests who have enjoyed a wedding, a school prom, anniversary or other special social affair…."

Much of the glamour came from the high-profile guests, especially from the burgeoning aviation industry. During an era when there were no respectable hotels near the Cleveland Airport, and no highways to connect the airport efficiently with downtown Cleveland, the Westlake became "the place" for aviation leaders to stay. A natural place, too, since the pilots saw the hotel and its prominent signage from the air on their approach to the airport.

Aviation legends Jimmy Doolittle, Amelia Earhart, Charles Lindbergh and Eddie Rickenbacker either overnighted or dined at the Westlake, while in Cleveland for air race events or other reasons. At the time, these were some of the most famous people in the United States. General Doolittle made the first cross-country flight in an Airco DH 4 plane and was renowned for his daredevil tactics. Amelia Earhart flew solo across the Atlantic Ocean – the first woman to do so. Lucky Lindy had a long list of achievements including the first solo flight from New York to Paris. Rickenbacker was a decorated World War I hero.

The National Air Races were held in Cleveland most years from 1929 to 1949 except for during the world war. The business leaders who spearheaded those races were Frederick Crawford of Thompson Products, later TRW, and Louis Greve of Cleveland Pneumatic Tool Company. A number of the historic airplanes from these races can be seen at the Crawford Auto Aviation Collection in Cleveland. In the early 1930s, the Betsy Ross Aviators – an organization of female pilots available for military flight missions when needed – met at the Hotel Westlake as did the Ninety Nines women aviators group. Many commercial pilots and flight attendants also stayed there and then crossed the street to Candyland to purchase sweet treats or cigars. In a largely rural community, it was eye-opening for residents to see uniformed pilots and elegant flight attendants in their hometown.

On June 7, 1925, *The Plain Dealer* not only covered the grand opening of the Westlake, calling it "Greater Cleveland's Pre-Eminent Apartment Hotel," but also published a special advertising section celebrating the property. Advertisers included Lowenberg & Lowenberg Architects, American Enameled Products, Clifton Park Lumber, The Cleveland Metal Roofing & Ceiling Co., George Rackel & Sons, A.T. Westropp Decorating, Rhinelander Refrigerator Co., State Chemical, Henkel & Best Lighting Fixtures, The Murphy-in-a-Dor Bed (sic), and Ingersoll Hardware.

"There is no service which a commercial hotel offers guests that the Westlake does not provide," an accompanying article stated, noting the dearth of large hotels on the West side of Cleveland. It said the rooms were "restful to the eye and harmonious." The hotel rooms and apartments were furnished with everything a resident could want save for a piano, radio or phonograph (though renters were also welcome to bring their own furniture). The original manager at the Westlake was Sebastian Newman, who had begun his career in Brussels. He later worked in London and in Chicago, where he worked at the prestigious Palmer House and Congress Hotels. Newman was so endearing to clients that 25 families had moved into the Westlake even before the main entrance was accessible. The article also referenced the Corinthian Yacht Club, led by James W. Fraser of Lakewood, leasing 5,000 square feet in the basement facing the river. The leased space was subdivided into a lounge, club room, card room, and locker rooms. The article said that Fraser had hoped to base his club on the nearby island, but the Cleveland Yachting Club secured the rights to that property.

The good times lasted for a number of years but the Great Depression forced the property into bankruptcy in 1931, and some of the lavish touches were discontinued, such as the beautiful gardens behind the building. It was auctioned in 1935 for $151,000 – a fraction of its previously estimated value. But it remained an upscale hotel destination for some time thereafter. The elegant lower-level ballroom hosted countless weddings, anniversary parties, election-night gatherings, and convention banquets. During the patriotic days of World War II, the local American Legion post maintained a lighted sign showing the names of individuals serving in the military. A two-story, 140-car parking garage was added in 1953. In 1956, the property was offered for auction for $1 million but there no bidders.

The western-most front entrance led to the restaurant and lounge, which was not surprisingly called The Silverthorn. It was said to be the first and only cocktail lounge on the west side with air conditioning in the late 1930s.

A January 1962 fire did extensive damage both to the hotel property and its reputation, as did a ruptured tank valve that dumped 5,000 gallons of water onto the top floors just a few weeks later. New owners – Union Financial Corp. and Westlake Investment Co. – converted the facility to exclusively apartments and added an outdoor swimming pool. It remained a viable apartment complex for years to come. For example, when the Bry family relocated to Rocky River in the early-1960s, they stayed at the Westlake until they were able to move into their home.

Gradually, competing apartment complexes stole much of the Westlake's upscale business. At one point in the early 1970s, the City considered making the building into a 211-suite senior-living facility, until the federal funds needed for the project dried up. A July 22, 1973 *Plain Dealer* article said the hotel looked "like a Midwest matron in a New York singles bar." That article interviewed three long-term residents (a Mrs. O'Brien who had been there since 1933; Margaret Eyeman who moved in the same year; and Mrs. Mortimer Gibson, a resident since 1941) who recalled the property's glory days when residents got together throughout the year for festive parties. The article also interviewed Roneau Rush, 77, who evidently had been operating the basement valet since 1928.

By the late 1970s – when this writer spent two summers working at The Silverthorn as a kitchen and maintenance assistant – the Westlake had devolved into little more than a poorly maintained, oversize boarding house. The clientele at The Silverthorn was friendly and respectable, as restaurant owners Don and Ellen Mitten provided a hospitable environment and tasty food for guests. Occasional wedding receptions were still held in the ballroom, which was showing its age. Moreover, the building was in disrepair, and increasingly the residents included people down on their luck and drug dealers, while the ownership group was struggling financially.

Then came much-needed good news. In the early 1980s, developer Scott Mauer completely rehabilitated the Westlake, converting it to condominiums ranging from 900 to 2,500 square feet in size. The dingy white exterior was returned to the historic strawberry pink hue. Small rooms were expanded into larger suites. Penthouse level suites were added. The old ballroom was converted into three large suites. Plumbing and HVAC systems were replaced. The Silverthorn was converted into a party room available to residents. Once again, the property brought prestige to the area, attracting celebrities like actor Yul Brenner who stayed there in 1985 while performing in a play in Cleveland. The result, even 40 years later in the mid-2020s, is a highly attractive condominium complex, and the Westlake is once again one of the proud landmarks of Rocky River.

Figure 44 - The Westlake being renovated in 1983. (author's collection)

Figure 45 - The Westlake on a beautiful recent spring day. (author's collection)

The Mayor's Office

Rocky River has been led by a series of popularly elected mayors since 1903. Some have been more consequential than others, but each has contributed in some way to the development of this quintessential suburb.

Under the City's home rule charter adopted in 1960, the mayor, law director and Council members are all elected offices. Pamela Bobst is the Mayor and Michael O'Shea is the Law Director. The City Council President is David Furry. Furry is an at-large Council member as are Brian Sindelar and Christina Morris. The Council members elected by wards are Thomas Hunt (President Pro Tem), Mike O'Boyle, Jeanne Gallagher and Paul Shipp. The Clerk of Council is Sue Pease.

The first Mayor from 1903 to 1913 was Mark Mitchell, an English immigrant who ran a local blacksmith shop. In 1903, Mitchell oversaw the construction of the City's first jail. The project was put up for bid, and Mitchell didn't have to look far. The Van Dorn Iron Company, whose president lived in Rocky River, won the bid and assembled the small lockup. Mark resided for many years on Northview Road. Mark's son, Earl Mitchell, operated a wagon works and auto repair facility, and old photos suggest he operated out of the same building that housed his dad's business.

Sion Wenban succeeded Mitchell and was Mayor from 1913 until 1917. Wenban was one of the first two students to graduate from Lakewood High School in 1894, along with Walter Wagar. The hard-working young Wenban worked as a janitor, then as a grocery store clerk, and eventually had a business role with the Geiger and Keyse grocery store. He was involved in banking and managed the basket factory on Lake Road. In civic affairs, he was president of the Library Board and the Lakewood Park Cemetery Association. Wenban was the brother-in-law of John Hoag, a councilman and business leader. Wenban lived at 20012 Center Ridge Road, a lot now occupied by a commercial building. He died in 1951 and was buried in Lakewood Park Cemetery.

Carl Stein was Mayor of the village from 1917 to 1923 and then Mayor of the City from 1932 to 1941. Stein was the only individual to occupy the office when Rocky River was both a village and a city, and his combined 15 years of service made him one of the longest-serving Mayors. He was involved in restaurants (Rockcliffe Grill and Stein's in the Terminal Tower), banking, a nursery school (the Kiddie Club established in 1966), and in the women's-clothing wholesale business. Stein and his family lived in a large house at 2639 Wooster Road that dated to 1906 (and was converted into office space in 1990).

J.O. Gordon was mayor from 1923 to 1927 and historical accounts suggest that the financial administration was less than stellar during that period. Gordon left office with the City facing a financial quagmire.

Gordon was followed by Leonard Weitz, who held the office from 1927 to 1931 and oversaw the restoration of the City's fiscal soundness. An editorial in the *Cleveland News* indicated that "Rocky River is fortunate in having a Mayor of the Coolidge type, though he modestly gives the credit to the villagers who have supported his policies." The reference was to Calvin Coolidge who was serving as U.S. President through 1929. Rocky River became a City during Weitz's tenure in 1930.

After Stein's second run in the Mayor's office came Lyle Andrus, who had one of the shortest terms of service, just two years from 1941 to 1943.

He was followed from 1944 to 1949 by A. Richard Thomas. During his tenure, the City purchased the land for the City Hall campus, adopted a new master plan, and implemented a sweeping rezoning effort. In retrospect, this was one of the most consequential periods in the City. The land acquired then has been sufficient to allow for construction through the years of City Hall, police and fire facilities, Memorial Hall, the municipal pool, indoor skating rink, senior center and other facilities, all on the land acquired during the Thomas Administration.

J. Frank Gibson was Rocky River's Mayor throughout the 1950s. He operated a printing business in Lakewood as his "day job." It was at his encouragement that teacher Ralph Richards and student Ron Gable wrote a booklet on the history of Rocky River.

Joseph M. Poe served two terms, from 1960 to 1963. He was a Kenyon College graduate with a degree in English who next earned a law degree from Western Reserve Law School. A practicing attorney, his favorite hobbies included the breeding and racing of pigeons, raising roses, and performing with the Singers Club of Cleveland. The former mayor was living in Canal Fulton when he passed away in 2000 at the advanced age of 94.

Poe's successor was Norman Schwenk, a resident of 852 Elmwood Road near Elmwood Park.

Figure 46 - Mayor Schwenk's house as seen now at 852 Elmwood (courtesy of Zillow)

One of the red-letter dates in Schwenk's tenure was the opening of the Clifton Park Bridge. Schwenk represented Rocky River in the ribbon-cutting ceremony, standing alongside Lakewood Mayor Robert Lawther, Ohio Lieutenant Governor John Brown, and County Engineer Albert Porter. Schwenk served through 1967.

In the late 1960s, the mayor's races became unusually competitive. One of Schwenk's actions was to name City Councilman Earl Martin as services director. After Schwenk lost his re-election bid to Donald R. Patton in 1967, one of Patton's first actions was to fire Martin. (Two years later, Martin got revenge by winning the Mayor's race against Patton.) Patton was a survivor of the Battle of the Bulge who had moved from West Virginia to Ohio so his ailing son could receive treatment for cerebral palsy at the Cleveland Clinic. He wound up becoming the services director in Rocky River (much like his successors, Earl Martin and Don Umerley). Patton and his family lived in Ward One. After his lone term as Mayor of Rocky River, Patton left town. He worked for Polaroid in New Jersey and then moved to Utah, where he continued to practice his Mormon faith and got back into municipal services work. He ran unsuccessfully for mayor of Murray, Utah, in 1997. He died in that city in 2020 at the age of 94.

Earl Martin was the city's 13th mayor, and one of the most noteworthy, given his 23 years in office, from 1970 to 1993. He was elected eight different times. Martin was a Navy veteran with an entrepreneurial bent. He owned two gas stations early in his adult life, and in the late 1960s he opened the Martin's Corner convenience store, which is still going strong.

Martin's good business sense would serve him and the city well. Martin believed that the first roles of city government were to protect the citizens and provide outstanding services; those values guided his work. Under his leadership, emergency services response times improved, recycling was introduced, and the City acquired scooters for refuse collection, so that elderly residents didn't have to carry their trash cans to the curb (this was in the days when trash cans were made of metal and did not have wheels). His administration emphasized a commitment to quality services and every city employee was made to understand that commitment. This writer observed that practice first-hand while working two summers during college (1979 and 1980) for the City of Rocky River Service Department, which was led at that time by Artie Ritz, Tony Luce and his assistant, Dick Cornelius.

Back in 1971, Martin was also an enthusiastic advocate of the formation of the Westshore Council of Governments, an entity dedicated to sharing of resources and coordinating road projects among six western suburbs. It was the first such council in Cuyahoga County.

Mayor Martin finally lost a bit of his Midas touch in 1992. He was defeated by Martin Hoke of Lakewood for the GOP nomination for Congress (the enterprising Hoke then went on to defeat Mary Rose Oakar). Martin also advanced a controversial plan that would have converted a 150-bed hotel on Center Ridge Road into a jail to house prisoners from several western suburbs. The plan encountered vehement citizen opposition and was abandoned. The Mayor opted not to seek re-election later that year. Martin thereafter enjoyed an active retirement, spending time with family, playing gin rummy, and pursuing other interests, from 1993 until his death in 2019 at the age of 89. He resided in his later years at 21146 Lake Road. He was an ardent member of the GOP and the final sentences of his death notice were: "Make America Great Again. Vote Republican." Politics, it turned out, ran in the family. His son, Earl, later served as a state representative.

Martin's successor was the affable Don Umerley, who served five terms as Mayor. This was a very smooth transition, since Umerley had been in Martin's inner circle as the services director. Highly popular with voters, Umerley passed away while in office just four days before Christmas in 2001. The city's outstanding civic center, which includes athletic facilities and activity rooms, is named for him. His son, Jim Umerley, held a senior position for the City and has served as a realtor at ERA Solutions Realty. His daughter, Sue, resides on Beach Cliff Boulevard.

City Council President William Knoble succeeded Umerley in 2001. He filled out the unexpired term, and then was elected twice on his own, serving from 2001 to 2006. Knoble, a graduate of Ohio Wesleyan University and resident of 18989 Schlather Lane, devoted nearly his whole adult life to service to Rocky River.

Figure 47 - The Knoble home at 18989 Schlather Lane (courtesy of Zillow)

Knoble served on the charter review commission and the board of zoning appeals, and was elected to the City Council 12 times. He was also a 52-year member of Rocky River Presbyterian Church. As Mayor, Knoble focused on City finances, economic development and the continued professionalization of the fine staff. In 2006, Knoble resigned. In retirement, he enjoyed a trip to Israel and volunteered at the Beck Center and Business Advisors of Cleveland. Knoble passed away at age 80 in 2019.

The mayor since 2006 has been Pamela Bobst, who was City Council Chair at the time that Knoble resigned. Bobst, who has a master's degree in community health education from Kent State University, had been on the Council since 1996. Under Mayor Bobst's strong leadership, the City has continued to focus on excellent services and has planned for the future with studies of future development options. In 2018, she was one of 30 Mayors – and only 2 from Ohio – who met with President Trump at the White House to discuss the opioid crisis, infrastructure needs, and the economy. Popular with the voters, the hard-working Mayor has also interacted intentionally with the City's employees to continue to make the City a great place to work. She is married to optometrist Thomas Bobst, with whom she raised three children. The couple resides on Avalon Drive.

Neighbors to the West: Bay Village and Westlake

Rocky River's neighbors to the west are the fine cities of Bay Village and Westlake. Initially, these communities were part of Dover Township, along with North Olmsted. Bay Village became an independent village in 1901 and a city in 1950. North Olmsted broke away from Dover Township in 1912. The remaining area south of Bay Village was still known as Dover Township until 1940, when it changed its name to Westlake to avoid confusion with the then-larger city of Dover near New Philadelphia in Tuscarawas County, Ohio.

Today, Bay Village has a population of about 15,200 and Westlake has nearly 34,000 residents. This chapter will look at the fascinating history first of Bay Village, then Westlake.

The first prominent settler in today's Bay Village was Joseph Cahoon in 1810. The difficult trip from Vermont had taken six weeks but within four days of arriving, his family had built a cabin that would be their home for 117 years! They quickly planted seeds for apple and peach trees. For income, they operated a mill for grinding grain into flour and a distillery for making peach brandy. Life for the most part was quiet, but in 1813, the family heard loud gunfire and wondered if the United States, then under the leadership of President James Madison, was at war. They later learned the sound was from Commodore Perry's successful efforts in the Battle of Lake Erie.

Generations of Cahoon family members lived on the property. By 1917, the farm became a Bay Village park and the family's books helped start the Bay Village Library, which was in the family cabin until 1960. Since then, the cabin has served as the Rose Hill Museum. The City Hall was built on land the Cahoons donated. An 1882 barn owned by the Cahoons is part of a community center complex.

When one drives along Lake Road in Bay Village, there is a small cemetery. This dates back to 1814, when Rebecca Porter and her young son drowned in Lake Erie when trying to return by boat from Cleveland. There are 270 people buried at the spot that was donated by Mrs. Porter's husband, and it is known today as Lakeside Cemetery. Ida Maria Cahoon, who lived in Bay Village from 1852 to 1917, is among those buried at the site.

One of the pivotal figures in Bay Village history was John Huntington, an inventor and businessman. He was a cofounder of Standard Oil, an executive at the Cleveland Stone Company, owner of a fleet of ships, and a member of the Cleveland City Council. He bought 100 acres of lakefront property in Dover and built a lavish Victorian summer cottage. A water tower that he built to pump Lake Erie water over to his gardens, vineyard, and orchards for irrigation remarkably is still standing.

Figure 48 - Huntington Water Tower (courtesy of Cleveland State Library Special Collections)

Huntington passed away in 1893 at the age of 61. The Huntington family home burned down in 1920, and his estate sold the valuable lakefront property to MetroParks in 1925 for $500,000.

Huntington Beach is today one of the most popular beaches in Northeast Ohio, especially on summer weekends when people come by to lie in the sand, swim in the lake, toss footballs or frisbees, and enjoy refreshments and snacks that are sold onsite. Nearby, the BayArts program, formerly known as BayCrafters, was founded in 1948 and provides arts education and related programming.

The Nature and Science Center on Wolf Road is also on former Huntington family property. That museum was started in 1945 by a lady named Elberta Fleming. According to *Westlife* newspaper, she spent 15 years building a personal collection of animals and raising funds to establish a legitimate museum and nature center. Many a child and adult has enjoyed the center's programs. There is also a planetarium nearby.

Another Bay Village landmark has long been the former Bay View Hospital building at 23200 Lake Road, not far from the Rocky River border. This lakefront structure was originally a 10-bedroom mansion owned by Washington Lawrence, who had purchased 125 acres in about 1864. Lawrence had become wealthy in various manufacturing fields including sewing machines, bolts, and as the first president of the National Carbon Company (later Union Carbide) in Lakewood, which was the largest carbon factory in the world at that point. His company made the first mass-produced dry-cell batteries used in early phones. He also was an avid real-estate investor. He built a number of cottages which he leased to friends for summertime use and designated part of his acreage for a private golf course.

Lawrence and his wife had seven children, and he wanted a larger, all-stone home suitable for his large family and entertaining. According to a July 2011 article in *The Plain Dealer,* the home had a large hall, three sitting rooms, a library, dining room and kitchen on the main floor; eight bedrooms on the second floor; and a ballroom, sewing room, two bedrooms and a linen closet on the third floor. The family began residing there in 1900 even as construction continued, and one of Lawrence's daughters was married there that spring.

If the wedding was a high point, the remaining days of Lawrence's life were dismal. He sustained an arm injury while playing tennis that healed improperly, resulting in an amputation. He was overseeing the construction of his home's elevator shaft when he fell and sustained serious injuries. On top of these troubles came news from Chicago that the husband of another Lawrence daughter, who was living in the Windy City while the daughter stayed in Bay Village, was involved in an insurance-fraud and murder case. The story attracted unwanted national news coverage and brought shame to the family. Lawrence passed away at the age of 60 a short time later, having had little opportunity to enjoy the new house.

Figure 49 - Lawrence Mansion before it became a hospital (courtesy Bay Village Historical Society)

The remaining Lawrence family members lived in the mansion until the 1940s, when it was purchased by the Sheppard family, who used it for an osteopathic medicine hospital. Osteopathic medicine refers to a hands-on approach to diagnosing and treating health problems.

On July 4, 1954, as Ohioans were celebrating Independence Day and preparing for the night's fireworks shows, came the news that the wife of Dr. Sam Sheppard was murdered. Newspaper, television and radio news covered the incident intensely as the husband was charged with murder. A trial – during which it was revealed he had been having a three-year affair with a nurse – resulted in a conviction. Sheppard served jail time and was later acquitted in a second trial. Both cases attracted national attention. Even today, across the United States, when many people hear references to Bay Village, their minds immediately turn to the murder case. Despite all of the controversy and drama surrounding the 1954 murder, the hospital continued to operate until the late 1970s. In the early 1980s, the home-turned-hospital became the main building in the Cashelmara condominium complex.

Turning to Westlake, this was a spacious and heavily rural community well into the 1970s. The early industries included agriculture, potash, and mills. Leverett Johnson was one of the first to work the land in the future Westlake beginning in 1811. He built a cabin for himself and his wife, Abigail Cahoon, near today's intersection of Center Ridge Road and Porter Road. He went on to serve five terms in the Ohio General Assembly.

One of Mr. Johnson's contemporaries was Jedediah Crocker, a Revolutionary War veteran. The Crocker Park shopping center is on land he once owned. A 2,500 square-foot home built in 1853 by his son Sylvanus Crocker still stands at 29242 Detroit Road. A recent photo of Crocker's home is shown below.

Figure 50 - The 1853 Crocker home in Westlake (courtesy of Zillow)

The three Hall brothers were also early Dover Township residents, arriving as early as 1811. A home built by Charles Hall at 25360 Westwood Road also still survives. The abode dates back to 1833, making it one of the oldest structures on Cleveland's suburban west side.

The Clague Playhouse in Westlake, which provides delightful community theater every year, is located on land donated by Robert and Margaret Clague, who were immigrants from the Isle of Man, which is an island off the shore of Great Britain. Robert arrived in 1829 at the age of 22. He stayed for a number of weeks at the Sperry Inn on Center Ridge Road until his cabin was built. He and Margaret raised eight children in that cabin. His descendants, remaining in the area, built a brick home in 1876 that houses the Westlake Historical Society.

Westlake United Methodist Church at 27650 Center Ridge Road was founded in 1825. A church bell that dates to 1854 still rings every Sunday. Parishioners celebrated the church's bicentennial in September 2025.

In 1920, the population was only 1,754 people. With no highways connecting it with the employment center in Cleveland, it had not yet become a commuter center. But there were plenty of people passing through Westlake in the 1920s and 1930s, and they needed a place to get a night's sleep. In the days before motor lodges and motels were commonplace, many weary travelers overnighted at tourist camps. These camps were common across the country and one sometimes sees them depicted in Hollywood movies from that era. Schneider's Tourist Camp in Westlake opened in 1925 and continued operations into the 1930s. It was based near the intersection of Center Ridge Road and Dover Center Road. The small cottages included a bed, running water, a bathroom, and electric lights. Those who wished to cook had to do so in a community kitchen on the property.

Much like Rocky River, Westlake was home to a considerable number of greenhouses. One such greenhouse owner, Ray Perkins, opened his business in 1923 on Center Ridge Road and received a "Master Farmer" award from the Ohio Farm Bureau 10 years later.

By 1950, Westlake's population was approaching 5,000 people. Sewers had not yet been installed and Westlake did not officially become a city until 1957. The population grew 162 percent in the 1950s, but still stood at just 12,906 residents in 1960. It was not until the 1980s that Westlake surpassed Rocky River, Fairview Park and Bay Village in population.

Today, the largest employers in Westlake are Hyland Software, St. John Hospital Center, the local school district, TravelCenters of America and the Lutheran Home for the Aged, which has been in Westlake since 1932. Other companies doing business there are Scott Fetzer Corporation, and American Greetings, which relocated from Cleveland's west side to Brooklyn, and eventually to Westlake.

Rocky River Day

From the 1940s to the 1970s, the City government teamed up with the Rocky River Chamber of Commerce to present Rocky River Day. It was a fun, day-long celebration. Children eagerly awaited as gleaming red Rocky River fire trucks made their way down city streets, playing music and tossing wrapped candy, gum and lollipops. Children spent days decorating their bicycles, wagons, and making home-made floats to appear in the parade down Beach Cliff Boulevard and other streets. At Rocky River Park, local celebrities like Ron Penfound, the star of the Captain Penny children's television show on WEWS and PA announcer for the Cleveland Indians, added to the fun. There were hot dogs and burgers, a band performance at the bandstand, and an evening fireworks show.

Figure 51 - Jeff Windahl of Roslyn Drive at 1971 Rocky River Day (author's collection)

Following observations that a disproportionate share of the festivities were held in Ward One (the area around Lake Erie), the format was modified in the late 1970s and other approaches were tried. A "River City Sunday" event was planned but cancelled. In recent years, "River Day" has been held every July and has included classic car displays, an antique fair, live music, and the "Taste of Rocky River" event featuring local restaurants. The Chamber of Commerce remains integrally involved with the City in planning River Day. The well-received event has once again become a popular Rocky River tradition.

When Bowling Was Big

It's amazing how Americans' tastes in leisure activity change over time. In the early 1960s, there were more than 11,000 bowling alleys, and the Professional Bowling Association tour had a weekend network television show. By 2019, the total number of commercial bowling centers had declined to just over 4,000 and the bowling tour was no longer on network television.

The drop-off is evident in league play, which used to account for 75 percent of business, compared to today's estimated 35 percent. Bloomberg reported that in the 1970s, 9 million Americans were part of bowling leagues, a number that plunged to 1.34 million by 2018. Demographic and social trends have contributed to the decrease in the sport's popularity.

Another reason so many bowling alleys closed is increasing land values. This nationwide trend was evident in Rocky River. At one time, during the sport's peak, Rocky River residents had easy access to two bowling centers. Today, there are none.

River Lanes was located on the north side of Detroit Road, a convenient walk from the High School and the Junior High School. It was the smaller of the City's two bowling centers with 28 lanes and therefore had greater challenges to be profitable. It was eventually closed and was replaced by several retail stores on the same lot.

Westgate Lanes on Center Ridge Road, near the Fairview Park border, was the larger of the two bowling centers. It was on the PBA tour, hosting the renowned Northern Ohio Open into the early 1980s. During certain years, the tourney was named for its sponsors – Lawson's stores and Canada Dry soft drinks. Winners of that tournament included champion bowlers like Earl Anthony, Marshall Holman, Mark Roth, and Roy Buckley. Added attractions at the facility included a room of pool tables, snack shop and bar with large-screen television, plus ample pinball and video game machines.

Eventually, market forces caught up with Westgate Lanes, as well. The alley was torn down and the land was redeveloped. For those residents who still love to bowl, Buckeye Lanes in North Olmsted, Madison-Square Lanes in Lakewood, and Fairview Lanes in Fairview Park have bucked the odds and remained in operation.

A Civic Response to Drug Abuse

The need to discourage young people from abusing illegal drugs became a major concern across the country in the late Sixties and early Seventies. Between 1969 and 1971, music stars Jimi Hendrix, Janis Joplin, Brian Jones and Jim Morrison all suffered drug-related deaths while still in their twenties. Diane Linkletter, the daughter of popular television personality Art Linkletter, died by suicide after taking LSD in 1969. But the problem really hit home in Rocky River when a 15-year-old boy from the prosperous Tangletown neighborhood had to be hospitalized after an LSD-related drug trip.

The community responded with the formation of a civic group, the Rocky River Drug Action Committee. The goal was to educate the community and young people about the difference between drug use and drug abuse; and to dissuade young people from making dangerous choices and taking illegal drugs.

The leadership of the Drug Action Committee included its founding president, Eve Arslanian Kurkul, as well as Father Paul Plato from St. Christopher's Church, Reverend Weibrecht from one of the Methodist churches, attorney Jack Van Keuls, community leader Ellen Dimberg, and a representative of the Rocky River Police Department, among others. The group coordinated with the White House office of drug abuse prevention – which was headed at that time by Maureen Dean, the wife of White House Counsel John Dean – and other authorities to get the best educational materials into Rocky River and out to students, teachers and other civic groups.

In the years that followed, hard drug abuse (excluding marijuana) was rare, and no students lost their lives to drugs, suggesting that the Committee had a very positive impact. This Committee was formed and operated with the same public spirit that led to the formation of the Beach Cliff Biddies decades earlier when neighborhood ladies acted to prevent further drowning deaths. This community spirit has been seen time and again in Rocky River's history.

Even earlier concern for student welfare led to the tradition of the All-Night Party, beginning as early as the 1950s. This non-alcohol event was held on high school graduation night for all seniors, with the goal of helping them celebrate graduation in a safe and wholesome way. Parents spent weeks planning fun events and rehearsing skits that they performed on graduation night for the students. A meal and light refreshments were served. The party then moved to Rocky River Park for a bonfire on the beach and a conclusion to the celebration.

The City's Shortest Street

Perhaps the shortest street in Rocky River is Detour Avenue, which is a connector in two parts of the city. The northern-most version connects Stratford Drive and Beaconsfield Boulevard in the Beach Cliff Number Two neighborhood. There are no houses facing the short avenue, just the sides of four homes that face the streets that connect with Detour.

Residing in one of those four homes, on Beaconsfield, was Mr. Nichols, a dedicated yet gruff high school math teacher with a no-nonsense personality. The winter of 1977-1978 was one of the colder and snowier winters on record, complete with natural gas shortages that resulted in several days of school closures. The snowfalls kept coming, requiring the Rocky River services department to plow the new snow into ever-higher snow banks.

One Saturday evening in February 1978 at about 5:30 p.m., a Rocky River High School senior was driving home from a friend's house. The friend lived off of Center Ridge Road, and this senior lived in Tangletown. Driving north on Wagar Road, the senior turned right on Stratford, then left on Detour, with the plan to turn right on Beaconsfield as a shortcut. The road was slippery with fresh snow, and the car went into a skid, getting lodged in a massive snow bank right in front of the home of Mr. Nichols.

The senior had several friends living nearby and intended to simply walk over to one of their homes and borrow a snow shovel. Before he could do so, Mr. Nichols came huffing and puffing out of the side door of his house, pipe in mouth, snow shovel in hand, and mumbling something about revoking the student's driver's license. After about 10 or 15 minutes of collaborative shoveling the snow and shoving the car, the vehicle became dislodged. By the time the student could get out of the car and say thank you, Mr. Nichols was already huffing and puffing his way back into his house. Just another winter day in the life of Rocky River, and a lasting memory of the city's shortest street.

The Day Pro Wrestling Didn't Come to River

In the early-to-mid 1970s, professional wrestling was enjoying a surge of popularity. One syndicate was holding matches in Detroit and Akron, while sponsoring the "Big-Time Wrestling" show on Cleveland's Channel 61. Another syndicate, owned by Pedro Martinez and Johnny Powers, was staging matches at the Parma studios of Channel 43 as well as at the Cleveland Arena and in Buffalo.

During this era, an announcement aired that pro wrestling was coming to Rocky River High School for a Saturday afternoon card of wrestling action. As the date approached, a rumor was circulating that the event had been cancelled. In those days, there was no Internet to check for the status of an event, and in truth, one wouldn't even know who to call to verify the accuracy of the rumor.

Well aware of the cancellation rumor, two local boys, one a member of the Rocky River High School class of 1976 and the other a member of the class of 1978, rode their bicycles to the high school to see if the matches would still be held. Upon arrival, one look at the empty parking lot confirmed that there would be no wrestling. But just then, a man driving his car through the lot stopped and rolled down the window. Sure enough, it was George Dahmer, better known as Chief White Owl, one of the wrestlers on the original card. Evidently, he never received word of the cancellation and had driven to Rocky River from his home in Wilmington, Ohio, in vain. Nice enough though, he signed an autograph before driving off.

Research for this book on the Internet uncovered two interesting follow-up items on Chief White Owl. From a cashed check that was sold on EBay, one learns that the wrestler was paid $75 in June 1972 for a match. The front of the check from the Ameri-Can Wrestling Club was signed by John Powers. Dahmer had endorsed the back by signing, "Chief White Owl." Even with the inflation since the 1970s, and the fact that the matches were staged in advance, $75 does not seem like a lot of compensation for a wrestling appearance and getting one's body thrown around a ring. After all, if a wrestler appeared in eight matches per month at that level of compensation, the annual income would only have been $7,200 before taxes.

Dahmer was back in the news, sadly, in 2012. He had died in Florida in 2008, and four years later, a jury found the nursing home responsible for his care guilty of neglect which resulted in painful bedsores, the loss of his dentures and a fall from bed. The jury awarded Dahmer's estate almost $1.8 million in punitive damages. Following the verdict, his widow said her husband always tried to please the audience and never turned down an autograph request. Even with the frustration that he had driven three hours to Rocky River in vain, his one trip to the City was evidence of that claim.

The Fourth Generation of Rocky River Businesses (1950 to present)

The arrival of the 1950s saw Rocky River's evolution into a quintessential suburb quicken. New neighborhoods were developed, new investments were made in education, city services were expanded and a new generation of memorable businesses were launched. Gradually, additional business districts were developed: Further west on Detroit Road, on Lake Road near Kensington School, on Hilliard Boulevard, and on Center Ridge Road, among other locales. Farmland and greenhouses were repurposed for commercial and residential development. The 1950s and 1960s saw not only a wider variety of business enterprises, but entire shopping centers being developed to serve the needs of the growing, affluent community.

This chapter revisits some of the businesses from the period and the memorable individuals who ran them. Some of these enterprises are now just part of history while a select few are still in operation and thriving. We'll start with downtown Rocky River.

Downtown enterprises included Otto's Brauhaus restaurant, owned by the German immigrant Otto Fuchs. He owned the properties from 19064 to 19106 Detroit Road, which dated to the 1914 to 1920 period. The front of the restaurant featured the words "ein prosit der gemutlichkeit" loosely meaning, "A Toast to Well Being." Indeed, many hundreds of patrons stepped out of the restaurant well fed. A member of the Rocky River Masonic Lodge, Otto died in 2007 and was buried in Lakewood Park Cemetery.

Figure 52 - Otto's Brauhaus Restaurant as depicted in a postcard.

George Hamamjian started a popular art gallery and framing shop in 1970. The business survived the re-routing of downtown traffic on Old Detroit Road, and his son Ara has operated the shop since 1994. Around the corner, the Beach & Colahan appliance sales and service store served customers for many years at 19033 Detroit Road and was still going strong through the 1960s. There was a barber shop on Old Lake Road across from the Westlake Hotel where Cleveland Press editor Louis Seltzer and many other customers got their trims. On the corner of Old Detroit and Old Lake in the curved building was a dance studio owned by a couple who taught dance lessons together. They lived on Riverdale Road near the river and had children in the school system. The business had an arrangement with the school system to teach a Social Dancing class to fifth or sixth graders. Classes were held during the evening in a school gymnasium.

Across the street from the Westlake Condominiums in the early 1980s, Fragapane's Bakery offered some excellent breads and desserts. They later moved their operation to Westlake, but the neighborhood still had an option for sweet treats. In the mid-to-late1980s, an upscale ice cream shop called Mixins had a store across from the Westlake, which by now had been modernized and refurbished. Battersea Boulevard resident Kevin Jacques and his mother walked there one summer evening for a cone, and in walked Brook Jacoby and Mel Hall of the Cleveland Indians. One or both, Kevin speculates, was living at the Westlake that summer.

For many years, residents at the Westlake could get their dry cleaning done at a shop right within the luxury hotel. Hollywood Cleaners also operated in a narrow building right between the hotel parking lot and the railroad tracks. Nearby was Kyle Insurance at 19041 Detroit Road, as well as Ralph and Dorothy Schwartzenberg's family-owned floral shop. The Merritt-Phinney-Southard Realty agency was at 19284 Detroit Road in the 1960s.

Most long lasting of all of the downtown Rocky River stores perhaps was Ingersoll Hardware, which operated from 1906 to 2011, when Doug Yoder closed the family business. French immigrant Frank Ingersoll bought the business and the John Deere dealership from the previous owners, Geiger and Keyse. It was located at 19701 Old Detroit Road (the site of today's Mitchell Sotka's Antiques) before moving to 19333 Detroit Road. In the early days of this business, Frank Ingersoll acquired merchandise by riding into Cleveland on a horse-drawn wagon. He made purchases from the George Worthington Company hardware warehouse at 802 St. Clair Street or from other dealers in Cleveland. He would then make the same trip back, this time a bit slower since the horse was pulling far more weight. Frank and his family lived nearby on the southeast corner of Wooster Road and Telbir Avenue. One of Frank's two children was Charlie Ingersoll. According to a Rocky River Historical Society article by Gay Christensen-Dean, Charlie and his wife Ethel lived on Wooster Road on a lot gifted to them by Frank, the second lot north of Shoreland. Charlie bought his dad's John Deere dealership in 1927 and also distributed Gibson and Bolen tractors. He opened distributorships in several Ohio cities. Charlie also got involved in manufacturing products such as a spray to prevent flies from bothering cows and engine-driven power rollers that he sold to golf courses. Ingersoll also sold a root-washing machine that expedited the washing of vegetable crops.

In the Ingersoll store's later years, the Yoder family operated the enterprise. Doug Yoder's father was personally close to a number of area business leaders including Don Mitten, who ran the Silverthorn in the 1970s. Generations of Rocky Riverites relied on Ingersoll's for essential products for their farms, homes, yards, patios, gardens, businesses and construction projects. The Mellow Mushroom Pizza shop moved into the Ingersoll building on Detroit Road.

Nearby is the old train station at 19060 Depot Street. Beginning in 1964, it was owned by Norfolk & Western. That railroad merged with the Southern Railroad during the recession of 1982 to form the Norfolk Southern, which has owned the station ever since. (In 2025, Norfolk Southern announced a proposed merger with Union Pacific.) Norfolk & Western operated passenger trains until 1971, when Amtrak was established, and then concentrated exclusively on freight. For a time in the late 1970s, a railroad-themed restaurant called Victoria's Station did business near the train station. Prime rib, steaks, ribs and "Shrimp Victoria" were the menu mainstays. There were about 100 company-owned restaurants in this chain at its peak. By the time the holding company went bankrupt in 1986, the Rocky River restaurant was long gone.

Figure 53 - Victoria Station restaurant company logo.

Across the street from the train station for a number of decades was the Westlake Cab Company. Shoppers were delighted when Heinen's food store arrived in a nearby lot between Detroit Road and Wooster Road in the early 1970s. The upscale food store is still a staple in downtown Rocky River.

One of the popular current businesses on Lake Road is Cravings, which sells coffee, tea and Thai food. The building for many years housed Trio's Pizza, beginning in the 1970s. Trio's was a favorite for many teens and families. Nearby at 19765 Lake Road was a Shell service station that was under the same friendly ownership for decades. This was back when a service station not only sold gasoline and convenience items but also performed auto repairs. RRHS graduate Kate Prell did the business's accounting. Today, Nick's Auto Repair occupies the property.

Also south of Lake Road was Jim's Auto Body, a collision-repair shop owned by an argumentative raconteur who called himself "Diamond Jim." In one of the buildings formerly occupied by the Guy Cowan Pottery and the Barrett creamery, a business called Ro-LeC Metal Fabricators was doing business in the mid-1960s. Across the street at 19825 Lake Road until the 1970s was the Beach Cliff Nursery. This was a convenient place to buy seasonal shrubbery and flowers, and to pick out a Christmas tree every December. Locals were sad to see the enterprise close. Several cluster homes now stand on this lot.

Bearden's has been serving up steakburgers, onion rings and milkshakes on Lake Road since 1948. Loyal customers like Babs Hootman, who passed away in 2012 at age 84, visited regularly for decades. Young people often enjoyed late-evening visits to Bearden's after attending ballgames or movies. One of those young people, Steve Bailey of Lorain, later became a pitcher for the Cleveland Indians. Bailey met up with this author at Bearden's in 2006 for an interview for a book titled, "Portrait of a Franchise: An Intimate Look at Cleveland Indians Baseball in the Rockin' Sixties."

The Fourth Generation of Rocky River Businesses (1950 to present)

Figure 54 - Former Indians pitcher Steve Bailey with author Doug Kurkul at Bearden's Restaurant.

Earlier, the restaurant went by the name Jackson's and specialized in steak sandwiches and fried clams. Young and old customers alike have enjoyed watching the model railroad that circles the dining room just below ceiling level. The train dates back to when the restaurant was called Jackson's. The restaurant was operated by the Orange family until 2010, when it closed temporarily. Mr. Orange had two sons and one daughter working in the business, and for many years a friendly man nicknamed Stormin' Norman did much of the short-order cooking. New owner Jim Griffiths opened the refurbished Bearden's in 2011.

Just west of Bearden's on Lake Road was a brick building that was home to the publicly traded Lee Wilson Engineering Company. This company was a prominent builder of industrial furnaces and was credited with developing innovations in bell annealing, beginning in the 1930s. The company president, Lee Wilson, resided on Frazier Drive at Sunset Pointe and was a past CYC commodore.

In times past, most people filled prescriptions at community drug stores, where the pharmacist and the owner were the same person, rather than today's high-volume, less personal chain drug stores. Such was the case in Rocky River. Until the late 1960s when the owner retired, Scheer's Pharmacy on Lake Road across from Kensington School was the druggist of choice for many residents. Every August, as children prepared to return to classes, the school provided parents with a list of supplies the student would need – pencils, eraser, pens, ruler, Elmer's Glue, and the like. It was an annual ritual for children and parents to stop in at Scheer's and purchase that year's school supplies. Opening later in the same space was the Mardi Gras costume shop, which was in business for much of the 1970s. It always stretched the imagination to contemplate how a costume and novelty shop could make enough money year-around to stay in business in those days before e-commerce.

The other building across from Kensington School was constructed in the late 1920s. It included James Hardware, an old-style hardware store, where knowledgeable experts helped customers find exactly what they needed. A popular restaurant now occupies that space. Next door to James Hardware was Mike's Delicatessen. Mike, a European immigrant, had a small meat and cheese counter, but really could not compete with food stores. He seemed to do more business selling beer and soft drinks from his coolers, and peddling candy and baseball cards to neighborhood children. Kids who completed a purchase were offered two options for their change – coins or bubble gum. A novel way for Mike to make a little extra money.

On the far end of the row of shops was Theiss's (later Gene's) Bi-Rite Food Mart. Today, the Lake Road Market occupies this space. And in between Bi-Rite and Mike's Delicatessen was The Colonial Ice Cream Shoppe, a small store that sold ice cream cones, sports cards, gum and candy. When the owner went out of business around 1970, he cited "too much theft" as the reason. While that was undoubtedly a problem, competition from the two stores on either side of him, and other ice cream shops, certainly had to have been a factor. A Sinclair gas station occupied the small lot between the two commercial buildings.

Further west on Lake Road, near the Bay Village border, the Normandy senior apartment towers were constructed in 1967 and 1972 by land-developer Neville Chandler, the father of the sportscaster of the same name. The story behind the "Normandy" name is interesting. The elder Chandler had served as an intelligence officer in the U.S. Army in Algeria, Tunisia, Sicily, Rhineland, Ardennes, and Normandy. On an occasion after brutal conflict, Chandler and two colleagues were sent out in a jeep to determine the location of the enemy. While on this mission, they were captured and declared prisoners. Chandler observed the devastating losses on the German side including countless unburied casualties, and the discouraged demeanor of the captors.

As Carolyn and John Rowland explained in "*A History of the Normandy Apartments,* "Neville advised the Germans that his American command was poised to attack, but if the Germans would surrender to him, they would be treated as prisoners and provided with medical care and food and evacuated to safety." Incredibly, the small group of German officers decided to surrender. As the authors wrote, "Chandler returned to

France many times during his lifetime. He admired French architecture and style and it influenced many of his professional designs." It guided his choice for a name for his senior community, as well. Chandler's ownership group sold the property to Frank Celeste's NORCOR group in 1978. NORCOR struggled financially, and an S&L foreclosed on the property during the 1982 recession; the S&L sold it to Orlean Company in 1986.

Just west of today's Bradstreet's Landing Park, from the 1950s to the 1990s, stood the Harbor View Motel, at 22480 West Lake Road. When the single-level property opened, the owners touted it as Greater Cleveland's only lakefront motel complete with air conditioning. Located behind the beverage store with a sign visible from West Lake Road showing a lighthouse and a sailboat, the family-owned motel offered a sandy beach, access to the fishing pier, and a lakefront honeymoon suite. The motel is depicted in the postcard below. While some Rocky River residents with long memories mourn its loss, the beautiful Harbor Village Townhomes now occupy the site.

Figure 55 - Postcard depicting the Harbor View Motel. Photo by Harold Ingall (author's collection)

One of the longstanding businesses on Linda Street was Prasse Lumber. The company traced its history to 1897 in Cleveland. Three brothers – Charles, Emil and Manuel Prasse – established the enterprise and moved it to Rocky River. It made extensive use of the railroad spur to receive lumber deliveries. Generations of contractors and do-it-yourselfers relied on Prasse for their lumber needs. Beachcliff Cabinet & Design later occupied the building.

Prasse was across the railroad tracks from an outdoor community swimming pool and from the Henry J. Morgan American Legion Post 451, shown below. Although the address is 19911 Lake Road, the property is most easily accessed from Linda Street. The Post was established on January 11, 1934, during the Franklin Roosevelt Administration. Post 451 has hosted delicious spaghetti dinners, sponsored the organization's American Government, History & Americanism competition at RRHS, presented scholarships and annually sent two RRHS students to Buckeye Boys State where they learned first-hand about government. According to *The Congressional Record*, the Post had 300 members in 1999. The building remains and the Post is still active.

Figure 56 - American Legion Post 451, located off Linda Street. (author's collection)

The Fourth Generation of Rocky River Businesses (1950 to present)

Across from the Linda Shopping Center, Dawson's Insurance grew to 208 employees in three states. It was acquired by Assured Partners in 2012. Nearby at 19700 Detroit is the popular Mitchell's Ice Cream, which was renovated in 2025. Further south, the Linda Shopping Center was developed around 1960. It was formerly a sand pit and storage area operated by William R. Hoag, who sold coal and feed. The plaza, today called River Square, is now anchored by a Whole Foods Market. Ford's Clothiers has been there from the get-go, and it traces its roots back to 1913, when it opened on West 48th Street in Cleveland. For quality clothes and attentive service, it has always been a good bet. Ford's neighbor all these years has been Minotti's Wine Shop. Back in the 1970s, when beer can collecting became popular, the store stocked a wide variety of harder-to-find, regional beer brands. Fathers would happily try out the beer, while sons added the cans to their growing collections. Speaking of beer, the Linden Lounge was in this shopping center for many years, as well. The lounge was a good place for libation and had excellent food, too. A number of the workers from the City of Rocky River Service Department would get off of work at 3:30 p.m. and incredibly would be seated and served at the Linden Lounge less than 10 minutes later.

Marshall's Drug Store was one of the plaza's original anchors. Marshall's was one of the largest drugstore chains in the Midwest with about 50 stores. The founder was Wentworth Marshall, who was married to Louise Marie Gehring, a member of a famous brewing family in Cleveland. The store later became Cunningham's 21 Drugstore.

Michael's Family Restaurant was a popular spot for a meal that was almost like home-cooking. The owner, Michael Patrakkas, was an immigrant from the Greek island of

Crete. He never lost his appreciation for the opportunities the United States offered him, and he made headlines every holiday season by providing free meals to all customers on Thanksgiving Day. After 42 years of business, Michael's closed in 2019.

Also in the Linda Shopping Center for many years was a four-chair barber shop. The barbers were old pro's with mostly serious dispositions. One summer afternoon around 1980, when two of the barbers were killing time in front of the empty shop, two college-age boys drove by. The one with the longer, shoulder-length hair yelled, "Hey, how's business?" The barbers were not amused.

That shop's primary competition was probably Dugan's Barber Shop at 19248 Detroit Road, near the Beachcliff Theater. John Dugan lived in the house behind the store starting in 1962 and operated the business for several decades. Dugan's usually had only two or three barbers, but kept their clientele entertained with corny jokes, sports conversation, and antics like throwing cut hair at one another.

John Dugan's son, Bob Dugan, lived in the house for decades. His day job was an engineering position with Gould Inc., a manufacturer of auto, industrial and military parts. But he also had a part-time job in the evenings for almost a decade, managing the 1,546 seat Beach Cliff Theater. This Rocky River landmark based in an art deco building operated from 1937 to 1976. It opened on Saturday, August 28, 1937 with the movie, "Sing and Be Happy" starring Tony Martin and Leah Ray – the same day that Toyota Motors was established in Japan. The Beach Cliff was said by some to be the first theater on the west side of Cleveland to have an electronic marquee.

Today, the original theater is now part of the Beach Cliff Market Square shopping facility which includes a variety of delightful stores and restaurants. The Burntwood Tavern within the old theater space attempts to remain true to the building's history, even as it provides outstanding food, coffee and other beverages. The Pearl of the Orient Chinese restaurant operated in this complex from 1984 until 2019, when George Hwang opted not to renew his lease. These days, other tenants making the locale come alive include First Watch, Erie Island Coffee, Hand and Stone, Venetian Nail Spa, and the Goddard School.

Next door to the Market Square was Jan Dell Florist, which until recently had been in business since 1945. The flower shop, run by Jim Lewis, also sold Lionel, Kato and other model railroad cars and supplies to serve train enthusiasts.

To the west of River Square is Herb's Tavern, a Rocky River landmark. It was owned for more than 50 years by Herb and Bobbie Brugh, and was later operated by daughter Kim Brugh, a RRHS alumnus. Herb Brugh graduated from Heidelberg College, where he met Bobbie. The couple operated Herb's and lived on the second floor of the restaurant with two young children, until they saved up enough money to purchase a home.

Figure 57 - Herb's Tavern on a recent summer day. (author's collection)

As time went on, the Brugh's operated four different restaurants. Customers like sportswriter Dan Coughlin and hundreds of others loved to stop in for a beer, a HerbBurger, and friendly banter. Herb, who passed away in 2019, enjoyed hobbies including boating, woodworking, travel and collecting beer steins.

Nearby is Leo Luck's Auto Repairs at 19985 Detroit Road. The business, which dates to 1970, has serviced countless domestic, foreign and classic cars. Today, its neighbors include Soothe Massage, Kelsey Elizabeth's Cakes, and Elon Studios. On the corner of Detroit Road and Smith Court was a Baskin-Robbins ice cream store owned by the Bell family. Today, a three-story office complex occupies that space.

At 1260 Smith Court was the office of accountant Myron Xenos, a lifetime Rocky Riverite and nationally known rare-coin and antique expert. In 1956, at the age of 18, Xenos won third prize in the Fifth International Philatelic Exhibition (FIPEX) in New York City for his excellent stamp collection. Xenos resided on Higley Road. His commercial property on Smith Court, originally built in 1917, was advertised for sale in 2025 for a price of $350,000. Xenos, a former Finance Director for the City of Rocky River, passed away on July 20, 2025 at age 86, Across the street at 1259 Smith Court,

Ameriprise Financial occupies a 1924 structure that also was once a private home. The Rocky River Chamber of Commerce is nearby at 1236 Smith Court.

Further west on Detroit Road was J.L. Hecht, a lighting retailer. One RRHS student briefly had a part-time job at J.L. Hecht in the late 1970s, which ended quickly when he dropped a fragile glass chandelier from a ladder onto the floor. Another retailer, Ace Hardware, now occupies that edifice and ironically, that same student, now an adult, has shopped there.

Nearby is Martin's Corner Deli, a convenient food store operated by the family of former mayor Earl Martin. Thousands of customers have stopped in at Martin's Corner over the years, including NBA player Danny Ferry and baseball star Travis Hafner. Still further west on Detroit Road where today there is a senior-care apartment, for many years the Rocky River Flower Shop did business.

To the south, Hilliard Boulevard has fewer retail establishments, since Magnificat High School, a couple of churches, and the City Hall campus take up so much of the real estate frontage. One popular establishment still around is Bucci's Pizza. There was also a Lawson's Milk store until the late 1970s, selling milk, Big O orange juice, beer, liverwurst, chipped chop ham, chip dip, and other products. To see a Lawson's store these days, you'll have to visit China or Japan. Murman's Super Value was a food store on Hilliard until 1975, when that business closed and the U.S. Post Office moved into the brick building. The Hilliard-Wooster Beverage store was nearby at 19232 Hilliard Boulevard, offering "service to your car" in the 1960s.

At 2244 Wooster Road, Burgoyne's Sporting Goods was a good place to pick up ice skates, sneakers, tennis rackets, and other sports gear. Other nearby businesses on Wooster Road included the Koch School of Music which opened in 1952, the long established Kiddie Klub Nursery School, and the RockCliff Grill, which at various times was also known as Pat Joyce's, DaVinci's, and The Colony.

Another interesting establishment was the medical office of a well-known physician named Dr. Leslie S. Dean at 1982 Wooster Road. The medical clinic was part of his home, which he shared with his wife Reba Harbison Dean and two sons. This was an old-style practice, operating for more than 40 years since 1931. There was a side entrance, leading to a small (and often crowded) waiting room – no social distancing here. There was a small exam room, alongside two closets that were used as medication-storage rooms. Pills and throat lozenges by the thousands were stored in big glass jugs. He sold the pills personally, he indicated, to save his patients money. Dr. Dean, who was born on January 29, 1899, was a believer in the power of penicillin, which he dispensed by shots.

Figure 58 - The former Wooster Road office of Dr. Dean (author's collection)

Through the years, Dr. Dean helped hundreds of patients feel better every month. But his way of practicing, which included seeing up to 50 patients per day, ran into conflict with the law, and an undercover investigation from 1971 to 1973. For a time, he was administering methadone to recovering heroin addicts but stopped after the Rocky River Police Department objected to the clientele his practice was attracting. Furthermore, the renowned reporter George Condon of *The Plain Dealer* investigated his practice. In 1974 Dr. Dean was indicted on seven counts of violating a state drug law: Administering amphetamines and barbiturates without a physical examination or medical history. An unnamed police spokesperson at the time said that Dr. Dean was a well-meaning physician whose time had passed. At some point, Dean closed his practice; the Internet does not yield any information about the final outcome of the charges against him. But one of his sons, also a physician, explained to those who would listen that the authorities and media had not been entirely fair with his dad. The elder Dr. Dean passed away on October 3, 1982 and is buried next to his wife at the historic Dean family cemetery in Jamestown, Ohio.

Further south, Center Ridge Road in 1953 was heavily devoted to tomato farms. Gradually, commercial enterprises sprang up including the recently closed Rustic Restaurant, a long-gone drive-in movie theater, and Szabo's Shoes. Szabo's had been there 66 years when it closed in 2019. Ulric Szabo, age 44, said he shuttered the business because online shopping and liberal return policies were making it hard to remain profitable. Since he owned the building, he was able to lease it out. It was a case, so to speak, of in with Zappos, out with Szabo's.

Frank Drellishak was a mechanic who after losing two fingers on his right hand decided it was time to own an auto-repair business and employ his family members. He commenced business in 1945 providing service not only to automobiles, but also tractors and open-air delivery trucks from greenhouses and truck gardens. In 1988, his son moved the business to the current location on Center Ridge with eight bays, in a former General Tire facility.

Westgate Shopping Center was built in the 1950s, then converted to an indoor mall in the early 1970s. Nowadays, indoor malls are out of fashion, and it's back to being a shopping plaza, with a different name. "If you live long enough," said one wag, "you'll see trends like that go back and forth several times in your lifetime." Anchor stores early on included Higbee's, Halle's, Stouffer's Restaurant, and Federal's Department Store. Federal's was a regional chain selling clothing and household items, established in Detroit in 1929. It went bankrupt in 1972. Shuttler's Men's Wear at Westgate was an alternate choice for buying a suit or renting a tuxedo.

The shopping center included Kresge's "dime store." Kresge's was a chain of five-and-dime stores with lunch counters that was established in 1897 with the first store in Memphis. By 1940 there were 682 such stores. You could buy an endless array of items there, even pet turtles, hamsters, and goldfish. The Kresge's in Rocky River lasted until the late 1970s; the parent company eventually morphed into K-Mart.

Across the street from Westgate was Manner's Big Boy restaurant. Manner's was one of a number of franchisees that operated the casual, dine-in Big Boys restaurants. In Rocky River, one of their most loyal customers was Sunny Christensen, the greenhouse operator, who ate lunch there often. Because his clothes would be dirty from his work, he reached an arrangement to allow him to eat his lunches in the kitchen! Nationally, the first Big Boy restaurant was established in 1936 in Glendale, California. The menus typically included over-sized burgers, fried chicken, pasta meals, and the "brawny lad" sandwich (which used a rye bun).

On the south side of Center Ridge Road these days, west of Wagar Road, is the RTA bus terminal. This attractive, functional facility was designed by none other than architect Joseph Shaffer, a 1978 RRHS graduate.

Near where the Firestone auto-care center is today, Grabowski Music Company was a great place to purchase a piano, organ, guitar or sheet music in the 1960s. Nearby, Johnny's Barber Shop had three barbers working at 19637 Center Ridge Road. Their slogan was "We need your head to run our business." South of Center Ridge Road, Master Pizza was a popular spot during the 1970s for pizza, Italian food and a jukebox that cost just 10 cents per song. The Rocky River Master Pizza closed around 1980, but other branches remained open, and in 2020, the chain returned to Lakewood.

The Fourth Generation of Rocky River Businesses (1950 to present)

On Center Ridge Road to the west is the River Plaza shopping center. For many years it was anchored by Uncle Bill's, a discount department store that sold everything from clothing and shoes to sporting goods, records, books, hardware and home furnishings. The chain was established in 1955 by Sidney Axelrod and was sold to Cook's Coffee Company in 1961. The Rocky River site is now occupied by a large food store. River Plaza also featured a medium-size Olson Electronics store, which at the time was a competitor of RadioShack.

This plaza was also home to Schwede's Appliance Village, which was a popular retail establishment. The store was badly damaged by a fire, and authorities brought arson charges against owner Ray Schwede, a resident of Frazier Drive. A trial was held and Schwede was found not guilty. The verdict came as no surprise to neighbors who long respected Ray, a U.S. Navy aviator, 14-year Rocky River City Councilman and business leader. He and wife Jayne were married for an amazing 63 years.

Also on Center Ridge Road, John Marquard Sons was a land-development company. The elder Marquard started in construction and had five sons, all involved in the family business. By the early 1960s, they developed East Surrey and West Surrey Court, along with Tonawanda Drive and Laramie Drive, all south of Hilliard Boulevard. Much of the land had been owned by Dan Gardner.

Stadler's Jewelry is a family-owned business that moved to Rocky River in 1968 after countless robberies at their unsafe Cleveland location on West 58th Street and Detroit Road. They have been at their current location at 20502 Center Ridge Road since 1980.

The Rockport Shopping Center on Center Ridge Road in eastern Rocky River saw growth in the late 1960s and 1970s. This center was built on farmland formerly owned by businessman William Hoag. Anchoring the shopping center, Forest City was a hardware store and lumber center with a large footprint. At its peak, Forest City operated 20 retail outlets but the Ratner family, which owned the business, got into real-estate management and development, and eventually abandoned the retail world. A movie theater and several small shops were just east of Forest City. A kind gentleman named Milton Kornman owned a Cleveland Stamp and Coin Company shop at the center and did all he could to encourage young people to pursue those hobbies. The Brown Derby operated a restaurant with one of Ohio's first salad bars on the left side of its facility, and a night club with a deejay spinning dance music on the right side. Another nearby restaurant was the Ponderosa Steakhouse, popular for its quick-service steaks and unlimited soft drinks.

Over time, the center was redeveloped as the Shops at Rockport. Recent and current tenants have included Fitworks, Storage Zone, Little Gym and Panera Bread. The Brighton Chase apartments, a $30 million residential development project, now occupies some of the center's original footprint.

Across the street for many years was a small shop called Eva's Boutique. It was run by Eva Grady, who escaped from Hungary with her husband and son (along with 200,000 other citizens) during the Hungarian Uprising against communism in 1956. Eva arrived in Rocky River, where she felt right at home with the large Hungarian-American population. She designed, produced and sold women's clothes and hosted fashion shows where local models displayed her creations. She was a consistent supporter of the Ursuline Sisters of Cleveland. Eva eventually moved to Naples, Florida, where she enjoyed a retirement full of tennis and beachcombing. She passed away at age 84 in 2015.

Also across the street from Rockport Shopping Center was a fast-food restaurant called Casey's Drive-In. In the late 1960s, the business arranged with the Cleveland Indians to have several of the Tribe's players make personal appearances. A promotion for Casey's and their "old-fashioned price days" follows below.

The Fourth Generation of Rocky River Businesses (1950 to present)

Figure 59 - One of the six Casey's Drive-In restaurants was on Center Ridge Road.

Rocky River has never been a primary location for auto dealerships, but at one time, Ed Stinn Chevrolet on the south side of Center Ridge Road (technically in Fairview Park) claimed to be Ohio's largest Chevrolet dealer using the tagline "the #1 team." Stinn filmed television commercials with former Indians pitcher and broadcaster Mudcat Grant. Stinn was said by some to have been involved in gambling and his business career ended with some bitterness. As one poster on the Internet alleged, "That place sat empty for a decade because ol' Ed had debts to people who don't refinance unless your kneecaps are part of the deal." He sold his business to Ganley Chevrolet but then wound up in protracted litigation with Ganley. He also was involved in a lawsuit involving National City Bank. Stinn passed away in 2005, followed by his wife, Barbara, in 2013.

The Old Austria Restaurant was operated on Center Ridge Road by Willy and Theresa Herzberger, European immigrants with a love to show their guests a good time. They retired from the restaurant business in 1979 and spent winters in Florida. Theresa passed away in 2016 at age 88.

Other memorable establishments on Center Ridge Road included Westgate Lanes bowling alley (see earlier chapter on bowling), the Westgate Motel, River Oaks Racquet Club, Arby's Restaurant (still present), Dominic's Pizza (still going strong), the Welsh Home (also still in operation), Mister Hero sub shop, Dante Lavelli's Appliances (owned by the Pro Football Hall of Famer), the United States Cast Metals Federation (which was comprised of several associations including the American Foundry Society), the Rocky River Pharmacy (which already had a drive-through window in the mid-1960s), and Ohliger Drugs, located at the corner of Wagar and Center Ridge which has since relocated to Westlake.

Rerouting Downtown

One summer day during 1978, the Rocky River Chamber of Commerce held a lunch meeting at The Silverthorn with guest speaker Ronald Stackhouse, the Cuyahoga County Engineer. Stackhouse was a Republican, in his first and only term in that office. This was back in the days when Republicans still won county-wide office in Cuyahoga County with some regularity.

There was a strong turnout for the lunch meeting, and with good reason. Stackhouse was there to explain a county road project that would reroute traffic in Rocky River and involve the construction of a new bridge across the Rocky River. Old Detroit Road in downtown Rocky River would become a one-way street, Stackhouse explained, and through traffic on Detroit would be routed past the downtown area toward the new bridge, which led to Lakewood.

Some business leaders in attendance were in opposition because it could mean less traffic past their business, but others argued that this plan was better than a previous proposal, pushed by former County Engineer Albert Porter, that would have widened Old Detroit Road and destroyed a number of downtown buildings. Still others on hand that day simply wanted to understand what was going to happen, and when.

The plan explained that day at The Silverthorn came to pass over the next couple of years, with the new bridge completed in 1980.

Civic Improvements

Part of what makes Rocky River a quintessential suburb is the City's long and ongoing record of civic improvements. The collective vision and dedication of generations of Mayors, City Council members, planning commission members, municipal workers, volunteers and voters have led to an array of well-maintained facilities.

The story starts with the Public Library. As early as 1877, during the Rutherford Hayes years, the North Ridge Literary Society contributed funds to purchase 345 books to start a library. The Society stopped meeting in 1902, but the books were placed in storage with confidence that some day a true library would emerge. In 1924, a lending library was established in a room in a schoolhouse and 912 registered guests borrowed books the first year. This was remarkable in a community of perhaps 3,000 people. Within two years, a board of trustees for a public library was established with Emily Macbeth as president and Harry Jacobs as secretary. A tax levy was approved and the Macbeth family contributed $25,000 for use in acquiring land and constructing the library, which opened in 1928.

In 1954, Sophia Schlather donated $100,000 to fund a new wing on the building's south side. Still, there was a need for more space to accommodate children's books and in 1972, voters approved a 20-year bond issue that doubled the square footage. In 1978, Maude Michael's donation allowed the library to purchase the John Brodbeck collection of Cowan pottery, made right in Rocky River. Further improvements were made through the years, including educational programs, swift embracement of Internet, and new-media resources. By 2002, the Rocky River Public Library was named the seventh best in the country by Hennen's American Public Library rating system. Today, the library is a vibrant educational, literary and cultural center at the heart of the City's quality of life.

One of the most visionary moves by City leaders was the purchase of the large tract of land at the corner of Wagar Road and Hilliard Boulevard. The new City Hall opened in 1954 after 45 years in a building downtown. Memorial Hall was built as a multi-purpose facility honoring those who gave their lives in the defense of our nation. Today, it is known as the Don Umerley Civic Center/Memorial Hall in memory of the former mayor. The Rocky River Municipal Court was established in 1958, serving five cities. Wisely, the land purchase included more acreage than was needed at the time. City leaders anticipated that a growing community would have future needs. Over the decades, the City added a large outdoor pool, indoor ice-skating rink, a senior citizens center, and an activities and recreation center. In 2020, the police station was remodeled to incorporate a "citizens' space" that Citizen Police Academy participants and other taxpayers can reserve for meetings and events.

The indoor ice rink was especially a step forward. Until its construction, residents had few options for skating. The City would pour water each year until the 1970s into the flat area used by local kids to play football and softball at Rocky River Park, and when temperatures were cold enough, it could accommodate dozens of skaters. A small structure with a cast iron stove allowed skaters to warm up for a few moments. The following greeting card painted by Louise Gallagher and offered by the Rocky River Historical Society for purchase shows ice skating at Rocky River Park with the old chalet in the background and the small stove house on the right.

Figure 60 - Louise Gallagher painting of Rocky River Park courtesy of Rocky River Historical Society. Greeting cards available through the Historical Society.

The indoor rink allows scheduled times for open skating, lessons, and high school hockey team practices and games. Teens ever since have enjoyed skating together there.

What is next in Rocky River in terms of civic improvements? Time will tell. The City periodically updates its master plan. Many ideas are on the table, and will be the subject of discussion and evaluation. If the future is anything like the past, there will be a continued commitment to meeting the needs of the community and ensuring a high quality of life.

Restoring the Clock Tower

When a clock tower was first constructed near Lake Road in 1912, it was intended as a gateway to welcome visitors to what was a developer's dream: A beautiful neighborhood of unique, quality homes within walking distance of Lake Erie and its breathtaking sunsets.

The Beach Cliff neighborhood grew around the clock tower, fulfilling the dreams of all who took an interest in the new community. Kensington School was constructed just opposite the clock tower 15 years later. The City bought the land around the clock tower in 1950. There the tower stood until 1956, when a windstorm leveled it to the ground. For 31 years, the small grassy area was empty, but people in Rocky River have long memories – in a positive way.

Figure 61 - Rocky River Clock Tower as seen in 2025 (author's collection)

So it was that in 1986, William (Hoot) Gibson, the son of former Mayor Gibson, launched a fundraising effort. A year later, a new tower went up, a replica of the original. But that is only part of the story. The other aspect is the maintenance of the tower and the garden area that surrounds it. That work is happily performed by members of the Beach Cliff Garden Club. The club celebrated its 95th anniversary in 2024. The group won a national achievement award in 2014. Its goals include not only the beautification of the area, but also to increase the understanding and appreciation for horticulture.

Neighbors to the South: Fairview Park

Rocky River's neighbor to the south is the fine city of Fairview Park. Both cities were once part of Rockport Township, and some of the early landowners' property was on both sides of today's boundary line. Even today, some residents cannot tell you where one municipality starts and one ends. And some school children in Fairview Park have been part of the Rocky River School District. It's therefore not surprising that some of the communities' history parallels one another.

In 1910, Fairview received its charter to become an individual village, breaking away from Rockport Township. At this time, Fairview was a rural community with about 300 residents. Electricity, gas, streetlights and water lines were installed over the coming years, setting the stage for eventual growth. According to Census data, the modest 1920 population of 642 boomed to 3,689 people by 1930. (Over the same 10-year period, Rocky River grew from 1,861 to 5,632 residents.)

In 1949, the official name was changed from Fairview to Fairview Park to distinguish it from another city in Ohio named Fairview, and also as a requisite to attract a post office. The village officially became a city in 1951. These events occurred as it was experiencing its next big growth spurt, as the population peaked in 1960 with 21,681 persons. The population in 2023 was estimated at just over 16,700 residents, reflecting the tendency in the United States to have smaller families, as well as the desire of some home-buyers to purchase newer homes in the exurbs.

In 1966, the boundaries of Fairview Park became larger (by 3,500 persons) with the annexation of the Parkview Village community. Parkview is the southern-most portion of today's Fairview Park. Parkview citizens initially voted down a proposed annexation in 1961, but the promise of sewers and reliable services helped grease the skids for a positive annexation vote later.

The major east-west corridor is Lorain Road, which progresses eastward into Cleveland to the 1927 Hope Memorial Bridge over the Cuyahoga River. It becomes Carnegie Avenue on the other side. In the opposite direction, Lorain Road surprisingly does not lead to Lorain, Ohio. Instead, it heads southwest toward Elyria. The corner of Lorain Road and West 222nd Street is historically significant. It was the location of the Spencer family home. Dating back to the 1850s and 1860s, there are some who believe that the farmhouse at that location was part of the Underground Railroad that helped slaves achieve freedom. The corner eventually became part of a busy commercial corridor and passersby seldom if ever think about the corner's legacy. The Fairview Park Shopping Center on Lorain Road was developed in the 1940s, followed by Westgate at the border with Rocky River on Center Ridge Road, in 1954.

One of the city's major employers has long been a hospital. The original hospital was founded in 1892 and was based on Franklin Avenue in Cleveland. It took the "Fairview" name in 1917 and moved to its present location in 1955. Since 1997, it has been part of the Cleveland Clinic system.

The city has had a number of outstanding mayors, and several had noteworthy achievements. David Bain was the mayor from 1932 to 1943. When the Interurban train stopped service in 1938, Fairview Park became the first city in Ohio with a municipally owned bus system. Also, in 1937, a city-owned cabin was constructed with the support of the Works Progress Administration (WPA). No sooner was it constructed than it burned down, however WPA helped fund a replacement cabin. Bain Park, and the Bain Park Cabin, are named in the former mayor's memory.

Karl Bohlken was one of the longest-serving mayors, and a park off of West 210th Street (Wagar Road) is named in his honor. Serving from 1944 to 1957, he presided over the development of both major shopping centers, as well as the 1957 dedication of the new city library. Bohlken's term of service ended when he was defeated for re-election in the 1956 Republican primary election.

The youngest mayor was Richard Anter, a former Fairview High School basketball star, who was only 28 years old when he was elected in 1980. Anter ran unsuccessfully for Congress as a Republican in 1982 against Rep. Ed Feighan, but thereafter turned his attention to economic development work, where he was involved in many of Greater Cleveland's key projects. He passed away in 2019.

In 2023, Fairview Park voters unseated an incumbent mayor and an incumbent council member. Bill Schneider, a political newcomer, is now the city's mayor, after narrowly beating Patrick Cooney. Following his defeat, Cooney credited the city's employees with helping secure a number of achievements during his tenure.

Another memorable citizen was Orrie Baumgardner, who was the fire chief from 1944 to 1973. He resided in a home at the corner of Lorain and West 204th Street. His trademark was the dalmatian dogs that would accompany him to the firehouse. Orrie was also a ham radio operator, and was the son of John Baumgardner, whose grocery store supplied much of the food enjoyed by Fairview residents for many years.

From the 1960s into the mid-1980s, Fairview Park was the home of Mike Garcia, a former pitching star for the Cleveland Indians. In 1954, Garcia led the American League in ERA, helping the club to the pennant. Through the late 1940s and much of the 1950s, he teamed with Bob Feller, Early Wynn and Bob Lemon to give the Indians the most intimidating pitching staff in the league. Beginning in 1955, he operated a dry-cleaning business in Parma, which became his full-time focus after he retired from baseball. Garcia was nicknamed the Big Bear, due to his dark hair and stout 220 pounds on a barrel-chested five-foot-eleven frame. Garcia, an adopted son of Fairview Park, was age 62 when he died of complications of diabetes and kidney disease in January of 1986.

The city's northern border is defined by Center Ridge Road, while the southern border is marked by Brook Park Road. Fairview Park is bordered on the west by North Olmsted, and to the south and east by the Metroparks system. Nearby Mastick Woods Golf Course is named for the Mastick family, large landholders in Rockport Township and the area that now encompasses Puritas Road in Cleveland.

Sports Figures Calling Rocky River Home

Befitting a quintessential suburb in close proximity to Cleveland, a large number of prominent sports figures have made Rocky River their home.

One of the best known was Joe Gordon, below, a member of the Baseball Hall of Fame. Joe played second base for the Indians from 1947 to 1950 and was one of the leading contributors to the 1948 Indians championship team. When the Indians activated Larry Doby as the first African American player in the American League, Gordon made a point to welcome Doby, play catch with him before games, and ensure that he felt welcome. During this time, Gordon lived on Purnell Road in Rocky River, west of Wooster Road. He was said to have been friendly with the neighbors and to have played stickball with young children on the street. Joe returned to the Indians as their manager in 1958 and guided the team to a strong second-place finish the following season.

Figure 62 - Second baseman Joe Gordon (courtesy of Cleveland Indians/Guardians)

Herb Score, the Indians pitching star from the 1950s whose career was cut short by injuries, later spent three decades as the popular voice of the Tribe on radio. Herb and his lovely bride, Nancy, resided on Roslyn Drive and raised their children there. On summer mornings, whenever the Indians were in town, Herb could be seen jogging through the neighborhood or driving his convertible down to the Cleveland Yachting Club, where he would swim laps in the pool. He was as friendly in person as he seemed on the air.

Living just a block from Herb Score on Buckingham Drive was the television voice of the Indians, Harry Jones. Jones, who had previously covered sports for a local newspaper, later did nightly sportscasts on WJW-Channel 8 News, hosted a Sunday sports radio show on WJW-850 AM, and briefly worked for the Indians as public relations director, before having a fallout with general manager Gabe Paul. Nev Chandler, whose dad developed the Normandy, called Indians and Browns games on the radio. He was a 1964 graduate of Rocky River High School. An insightful analyst and popular air personality, he was only 48 years old when he died of cancer in 1994. Joe Tait, who called the Cavaliers and Indians games on the radio, lived in Rocky River briefly after a divorce, staying at a motel on Center Ridge Road. Another sports media figure who lived in Rocky River was Pete Franklin, who anchored a nightly sports talk show on WERE-AM and later on WWWE-AM, where he boasted that his show was heard in 38 states and half of Canada. In an era before shock jocks became the norm, Franklin garnered a strong following with his humor, encyclopedic knowledge of sports, and willingness to mix it up with regular callers such as The Swami, The Prosecutor, the Canoga Park Creep, and Mister Know it All. Franklin, his wife and two children lived in an apartment in Rocky River.

Former NBA star Barry Clemens, who played for the Cavaliers for two seasons, resided in Tangletown for many years. This superb shooter played high school ball in Xenia, Ohio, and the college game at Ohio Wesleyan, where he was a small-college All-American. After concluding his pro career alongside Bill Walton in Portland, Clemens served as Senior Vice President for McDonald & Company brokerage, riding the bus to and from their downtown office. He continued to play basketball in area leagues, even after a hip replacement, for the love of the game. In early 1978, a group of Cleveland Browns players faced off against a team of Rocky River community leaders for a charity basketball game at Rocky River High School. The Browns players usually rolled to easy victories, but with Barry Clemens hitting long jump shots for the community leaders, the Rocky River team gave the Browns a run for their money.

Rocky Riverite Dick Furry was an Ohio State University hoops star. The Buckeyes were NCAA champions in 1960, scoring more than 90 points a game while surrendering on average fewer than 70 points. Jerry Lucas, Larry Siegfried, Mel Nowell, John Havlicek, and Joe Roberts were the starters and Furry was the first man off the bench. A longtime resident on Cornwall Road with his wife, daughter Carol and son David (currently the Rocky River City Council President), Furry was selected by the New York Knicks in the 1960 NBA draft.

Local resident John Hanna was a player and coach for the Cleveland Crusaders in the World Hockey Association. He later returned to his native Cape Breton Island, Novia Scotia, where he lived out the rest of his days. Carter Camper, who played for the NHL Bruins, was born in Rocky River and attended RRHS. Browns linebacker Tom Cousineau lived for a time at the Westlake Condominium. Quarterback Bernie Kosar, one of the most popular Browns players of all time, also lived at the Westlake during the 1980s, as did several Cleveland Indians players. Chris Hovan of the Minnesota Vikings grew up in Rocky River and attended St. Ignatius High School. Browns legend Dante Lavelli operated an appliance store on Center Ridge Road into the 1990s. As late as 2000, Lavelli, Herb Score and former Browns kicker Lou Groza – along with their wives – would get together for dinner. Former NFL star Anthony Gonzalez, later a

Republican congressman, also lived in Rocky River. He was a three-year letterman at Ohio State and later played wide receiver in the NFL.

Shipbuilding industry magnate George Steinbrenner, who later owned the New York Yankees, was at one time a Rocky River inhabitant. Although he gained a reputation for firing managers and being impatient (as spoofed on the Seinfeld TV show), there was another side of him that the public and the media rarely saw. The late George Garden, who owned the Garden Nursery, used to tell the story of his truck breaking down on Lake Road in Rocky River, and Steinbrenner kindly pulling over to pick him up and give him a ride. Steinbrenner and former Indians star Al Rosen tried to purchase the Indians from Vernon Stouffer in 1972. Stouffer instead sold the franchise to Nick Mileti, and Steinbrenner instead turned his attention to the Yankees. Baseball history may have unfolded very differently had Steinbrenner and Rosen gained control of the Indians.

Another Indians player, pitcher Chris Perez, rented a house in Rocky River decades later. Perez, who pitched for the Tribe until 2013, was living in River when he was arrested for accepting delivery of a package containing illegal drugs. The parcel was addressed to his pet dog. Perez made the American League All-Star team in 2011 and 2012, but his career was over in 2014 when he was still just 28 years old.

Rocky River was back in the news in recent years for a very happy reason. Red Gerard, who grew up in the City, became the first American to win a gold medal in snowboarding in the 2018 Olympics. Several snowboarding facilities around the country now bear Gerard's name.

Baseball great Joe DiMaggio is never known to have visited Rocky River, but for 20 years he was the pitchman for a product known as Mr. Coffee, which was based on a heating element designed in 1971 by inventor Edmund Abel, a Rocky River resident. Abel owned the patent for Mr. Coffee though he sold its rights to a Cleveland company, North American Systems, and drew little financial profit or public credit. Earlier, Abel developed remote-controlled drones for the U.S. military. A hero in his own right, Abel resided in Rocky River until his death at the age of 92 in 2014.

For so many Rocky Riverites, golf is a favorite vocation. Local golfers may not realize that some big-name celebrities have golfed in the City. Arnold Palmer, Bob Hope and Yogi Berra are among the memorable names that have golfed at Rocky River's Westwood Country Club, as did Bobby Jones, one of the most influential individuals in the history of the sport.

Given Rocky River's status as a quintessential suburb, it won't be the least bit surprising if it continues to attract or produce big-name athletes as residents or visitors in the years to come.

Sammy Kaye, Michael Stanley, the Arts and Media

Musician Sammy Kaye was born in Lakewood, Ohio, in 1910 with the name of Samuel Zarnocay. While attending RRHS as a member of the class of 1928, he was involved in the drama club, glee club, Riverlet publication, and serving as class president. He won the state high school championship in high hurdles and was part of a state-champion relay team. Those athletic heroics won him a scholarship to Ohio University in Athens.

He studied civil engineering in Athens, but a growing love for music captured more of his attention. He had already learned to play banjo, clarinet and saxophone. He formed a small musical ensemble to make money on the side called Sammy's Hot Peppers, playing weddings and fraternity dances. Building on that foundation, he changed his name, formed the Sammy Kaye Orchestra, and gradually added more musicians to his ensemble as their popularity grew. From the Cabin Club night spot and Statler Hilton in Cleveland, to gigs in Cincinnati and Pittsburgh, then on to the Commodore Hotel on East 42nd Street in New York in 1938, his orchestra's popularity boomed.

Kaye gravitated to what came to be known as "sweet music," the light, melodic tunes that contrasted with the more danceable numbers being performed by other big bands. The critics weren't always kind to him, but the public loved his records. In 1941, Kaye published *Sammy Kaye's Sunday Serenade of Songs and Poems,* and at that point, he was still just getting warmed up. He and Don Reid (of the Statler Brothers band) would soon co-write the song, "Remember Pearl Harbor," one of Kaye's most famous numbers, which reached number three on the popular music charts. Other favorites from Kaye included "The White Cliffs of Dover," "Harbor Lights," and "My Buddy."

NBC awarded Kaye his own radio show, which led to further record sales. Into the 1950s, he continued to score hits with records like "Wanderin." Television offered him further exposure. He developed close friendships with fellow celebrities like Glenn Miller, Jimmy Dorsey, Jackie Gleason, Richard Nixon and Ronald Reagan, often enjoying rounds of golf together.

Between 1937 and 1971, he is said to have recorded 1,300 songs. Kaye finally retired from conducting in 1987, handing over his baton to his friend Roger Thorpe. He died of cancer a short time later in Ridgewood, New Jersey. A visitation for Kaye was held at St. Christopher's Catholic Church in Rocky River, and he was buried in plots next to his parents at Lakewood Park Cemetery. A separate service was held for him at St. Jean de Baptiste Church in New York City. Kaye and Thorpe met when they were both on the same music bill in 1979. Kaye invited Thorpe to participate in an upcoming tour, and over time they became close friends. Thorpe has kept the sound of Sammy Kaye's music alive for several more decades.

Kaye married Ruth Knox Elden in 1940 but they never had children and divorced in 1956. Kaye's sister, who also grew up in Rocky River, later lived in Westlake, and was married to a gentleman who ran a service station in Rocky River at the southeast corner of Wooster Road and Hilliard Boulevard, according to Sunny Christensen. Sammy Kaye returned to Rocky River periodically to visit family and friends and when doing so, he worshipped at St. Christopher's, where he offered generous donations.

Figure 63 - Entertainer Sammy Kaye (courtesy of Wikipedia)

While Sammy Kaye was noted for a feature in his live shows called "So You Want to Lead a Band," Michael Stanley was revered for songs like the rock anthem, "Strike Up the Band."

Stanley's real name was Michal Stanley Gee. His father was Francis Stanley Gee, a WGAR-AM air personality who partnered with sportscaster Bob Neal in announcing Cleveland Browns games and was the voice of the Cleveland Barons hockey team for a number of years. Stanley's mother was a part-time librarian and substitute teacher in the Rocky River school system. Stanley was in the RRHS Class of 1966 and later recalled a RRHS speech and drama teacher named Miss Howe as making a major impression on him. The Gee family lived at 842 Morewood Parkway, south of the railroad tracks.

While still in high school, Stanley formed a band called The Scepters. It featured Stanley on guitar and vocals, Chuck Inglefield on drums, Chris Johns on lead guitar, Bill Lucas on rhythm guitar, Scott Wilkerson on bass, and Chuck Hackett on keyboards. Except for Hackett, who was from Parma, all of the other band members had ties to Rocky River.

Much like Sammy Kaye, Stanley was gifted in athletics. He received a college baseball scholarship to Hiram College, where he also played in a band called "Silk." In 1969, ABC Records released the album, "Smooth as Silk." His next two LPs, titled, "Michael Stanley" and "Friends and Legends," featured guest appearances by the likes of David Sanborn, Todd Rundgren and Joe Walsh. The early albums featured his baritone vocals, superb guitar work and thoughtfully written songs.

He formed the Michael Stanley Band (MSB) in 1974 and continued recording and performing with this group of musicians until their farewell concerts in 1986 at the Front Row Theater. In the early years, he shared vocals with Jonah Koslen. Later, Koslen left to pursue a solo career, and Kevin Raleigh shared vocal duties. Meantime, the band recorded such favorites as "Let's Get the Show on the Road," "Why Should Love Be this Way," "Promises," "Heartland," "Let's Hear It," "My Town," "Someone Like You," and MSB's biggest hit, "He Can't Love You," featuring Raleigh on lead vocals.

Figure 64 - Michael Stanley induction into RRHS Hall of Fame. At right is Eve Kurkul, president of the RRHS Alumni and Parents Association. (author's collection)

Figure 65 - The Michael Stanley Band in concert at Ashland University in 1982 (Photo: Shari Burley)

When MTV went on the air in 1981, MSB was one of the first 50 artists highlighted. Their popularity in Northeast Ohio was breathtaking, equivalent to Bob Seger in Detroit, John Mellencamp in Indiana, or Bruce Springsteen in New Jersey. There was a common thread to each of these artists' music. All four acts drew upon blue-collar roots to write and perform music that working people could relate to as they lived their lives and eagerly awaited the weekends.

For example, MSB lyrics that captured the working-class spirit included, "I don't need to be told by you. I don't need anyone bringing me down. I just need you to hold me. Try as hard as I might. I'll never need anyone more than I need you tonight." Or in another song, "It's good for the body and good for the soul, to now and then get a little out of control. So, cut the bullshit, play a little rock n roll."

MSB set a record at Blossom Music Center with more than 74,000 for a four-night stand; and another attendance record at the Richfield Coliseum. MSB toured with such acts as Bruce Springsteen, the Doobie Brothers, and Foreigner. During one double-bill at the Richfield Coliseum, MSB was the main act and the more widely known REO Speedwagon was the warmup band. Eddie Money was another performer who opened for MSB.

Although MSB never reached comparable levels of popularity nationally, Stanley was content to move on to other endeavors, including co-hosting a nightly television show in Cleveland and later a drive-time classic rock radio show. He continued to perform periodically with longtime musical friends until shortly before his death in 2021 at age 72.

The paths of Sammy Kaye and Michael Stanley intersected in 1984, when both were inducted into the inaugural class of the Rocky River High School Alumni Hall of Fame at an event at the Cleveland Yachting Club. Kaye was inducted posthumously while Stanley was on hand – thanks to an invitation from Chuck Inglefield – to receive the award from Rocky River High School Alumni & Parents Association President Eve Arslanian Kurkul.

Rocky River has enjoyed numerous other connections to the arts from cartoonists to painters to arts dealers. Ed Kuekes resided at 1280 Medfield Drive (near Rocky River Presbyterian Church) for 17 years and was active in several community organizations. Kuekes was the editorial cartoonist at *The Plain Dealer* from 1949 until his retirement in 1966. He won the Pulitzer Prize in 1953 for a political cartoon titled "Aftermath" that communicated the tragedy of American soldiers dying overseas even before they were old enough to vote.

AFTERMATH —FROM THE CLEVELAND PLAIN DEALER

A number of Kuekes's works were displayed at the May Show at the Cleveland Museum of Art. He also drew the Alice in Wonderland syndicated comic in 1934. In the 1950s, some of his cartoons appeared in *The Plain Dealer* sports section. Every year at Christmastime, his friends looked forward to receiving Christmas cards in which he provided a humorous illustration depicting what he and his wife had been up to during the year gone by. Kuekes passed away in 1987 at the age of 85. His 4,000 original cartoons are now maintained in a file that is 51 linear feet long at Syracuse University.

Another cartoonist, Art Sansom, also was a Rocky River resident. Originally a General Electric draftsman and engineer, Sansom began drawing the "Born Loser" comic strip in 1965. He received the National Cartoonists Society's Reuben Award for excellence in humor comic strips in 1987 and 1991. Sansom's son, Chip, began co-producing the strip with him in the mid-1980s. The elder Sansom died on July 4, 1991 and is buried at Lakewood Park Cemetery. Chip is a resident of Lakewood.

For a time, cartoonist Tom Wilson also resided in Rocky River. Wilson joined Cleveland-based American Greetings in 1955 and became Creative Director two years later. He played an integral role in developing the company's Soft Touch line of greeting cards. Wilson drew the Ziggy comic strip – which appeared in 500 daily papers – from 1971 to 1987, when he turned over the duties to his Cincinnati-based son, Tom Wilson, Jr.

Other noteworthy figures from the arts community who have called Rocky River their home include Anthony Van Rooy, who operates a gallery on Superior Avenue in Cleveland; painter Marilyn Phyllis, whose children attended RRHS; painter and art instructor Lori Daugstrup, who grew up on Beach Cliff Boulevard; painter Jeff Evans; watercolor artist Ruth Rea who resided on Avalon Drive and later in the Normandy; and Gray's Auctioneers founder Deba Gray. Local artwork has been offered for viewing and sale at Rocky River establishments including the River Gallery on Old Detroit Road; Off the Wall Gallery on Old Detroit Road; A Gallery West (which has been on Center Ridge Road since 1982); Daugstrup Fine Art Studio on Oak Road; the Art Gallery on Detroit Road; and Gestures on Linda Street, among others.

One of Greater Cleveland's great Christmas traditions that brought joy to thousands of children – Mr. Jingeling – had a Rocky River connection. In 1956, Walter Halle and an advertising agency began promoting the sale of children's Christmas toys by creating Mr. Jingeling, who was touted as the elf who held the keys to Santa's toy workshop. Policeman Thomas Moviel, the first Mr. Jingeling, brought along large keys from a local jail as props. He was quickly succeeded by local actor Max Ellis, whose twice-daily appearances on WEWS Channel 5 were a hit with children. Ellis died in 1964, and Karl Mackey, who ran the Lakewood Little Theatre, played the role that year.

Finally, in 1965, Rocky Riverite Earl Keyes – one of the original employees at Channel 5 and the producer of the Captain Penny show – became the longest-running Mr. Jingeling. It only seemed right that someone named "Keyes" would be "the Keeper of the Keys." He appeared on Halle's seventh floor until the store closed in 1982 and on Higbee's 10th floor until it closed in 1992. He made his last appearance in 1995 at Tower City. Keyes lived at 22430 Bartlett Drive, near Bates School, until shortly before his death from heart trouble in 2000. Keyes's trademark on Mr. Jingeling, shown below, expired at the U.S. Patent & Trademark Office in 1993.

Figure 66 - Expired trademark for Mr. Jingeling. (public domain)

Other noteworthy Rocky River High School students who went onto roles in the arts and media include broadcast journalist Martin Savidge (class of 1976), comic actor and writer Pat McCormick known for his role in "Smoky and the Bandit," (1945) and MTV veejay Nina Blackwood (1970). Kevin Barnes of the band Montreal also was a Rocky River resident as were M-105 air personality Gary Fletcher and award-winning television and comic book writer Brian Vaughan.

The arts remain an integral part of the fabric of the community throughout the year and especially during the annual Fall Arts Festival held in the Old Detroit shopping district. In 2025, the 16th annual festival was held, fulfilling Mayor Bobst's vision of cultivating the arts community in town. Festival attendees are able to see and purchase paintings, photographs, drawings, ceramics, sculptures and other art forms. Dozens of volunteers team up with the City to plan and execute the yearly event.

The Emerald Necklace

A much-appreciated aspect of Rocky River's status as a quintessential suburb is its access to the Metroparks system. The metropolitan park is easily accessible both from Rocky River and neighboring Lakewood and provides a perfect setting for hiking, bicycling, boating, fishing and other outdoor recreation.

William Stinchcomb, the park system's first director, believed that urban residents need regular access to nature, wilderness and wildlife. To make that more accessible, he acquired the lands needed to form a ring-shaped design of parkland that encircles Greater Cleveland. Boston's Emerald Necklace, developed by Frederick Law Olmsted, was the model, and Olmsted's sons were contracted to help replicate that park system in Northeast Ohio.

Working out of the Standard Building in Cleveland, Stinchcomb also oversaw the planting of many hundreds of trees in the 1920s and securing federal funding in the 1930s for park improvements. Stinchcomb held the Director position from 1922 to 1957 and was on hand for the 1958 dedication of the 30-foot-tall white monument in his honor. It is just south of the Rockcliff Lane entrance to the Rocky River Reservation.

Lakewood Park Cemetery

In the late 1800s, there was a log cabin on the south side of Detroit Road that belonged to a community leader named Flavius Dean. Flavius lived to the age of 91, passing away in 1927.

An interesting and irrepressible character to say the least, Flavius Dean had been a student at Western Reserve College, living at 2248 Murray Hill Road in Cleveland. He later became a grocer and educator in Rockport Township (Rocky River). Flavius understood the benefits of having influential friends who could help him achieve his goals. One friend was John D. Rockefeller. Another was Congressman Clifton Beach, and it is said that Dean persuaded Beach to provide the land upon which Beach School was built.

Dean's log cabin was located on what today is part of the 45 acres that since 1912 have constituted Lakewood Park Cemetery. It is a beautiful cemetery with flowering shrubs, hundreds of trees, and uniform memorial stones. An onsite mausoleum dates back to 1921. The office was constructed in 1957 and a maintenance facility was modernized in the 1990s. Records were computerized by 2011. One reason for the cemetery's stability through the decades has been the steady leadership of a responsible board of directors, and a caring staff team. As of 2025, the Board of Trustees was composed of David C. Harris, Kenneth Burney, Gregory Helms, Edward Delzani, Sean McGettrick and Scott W. Kermode. The office supervisor is Sandy Sill who is supported by an able administrative and landscaping staff. For 11 years, the office supervisor was David Zaylor, a popular former Rocky River Junior High School science teacher.

There is a mass grave at the cemetery with the remains of 84 persons. These individuals were formerly buried (between 1830 and 1900) at the Mars Wagar Cemetery in Lakewood (on land that is now a parking garage). After that cemetery fell into neglect in an increasingly urban area, arrangements were made in the mid-1950s to move those graves to Lakewood Park. Mars Wagar's own grave is next to the mass grave.

At least four former major league baseball players are buried at Lakewood Park. Larry Twitchell, a native Clevelander, was an outfielder from 1886 to 1894 for several clubs, including the Cleveland Spiders. He passed away in 1930. George Uhle was another Cleveland native. Highly successful, he pitched from 1919 to 1936, and spent more than half of his career with Cleveland. He won 26 games in 1923 and topped that achievement by winning 27 games in 1926. George pitched against the likes of Babe Ruth, Lou Gehrig and Ty Cobb. With Cleveland, his teammates included Hall of

Famers Tris Speaker and Stan Coveleski. George died in Lakewood in 1985 at the age of 86 after a 20-year battle with emphysema.

Figure 67 - Pitcher George Uhle (public domain)

Figure 68 - Pitcher Clint Brown (public domain)

Clint Brown pitched from 1928 to 1942, including two stints with the Indians. In 1934, Clint traveled to Japan, accompanied by his newlywed wife Mary, as part of a barnstorming tour. He was in the Tribe's starting rotation in the early 1930s but worked out of the bullpen for most of the rest of his big-league tenure. After baseball, Clint worked as a chicken farmer and when that proved unprofitable, he became a sales representative in the foundry industry. He died of a heart attack in Rocky River in 1955, just 52 years of age. When Mary passed away 41 years later, she was buried beside him.

Also buried here is Herb Score, the former pitcher and longtime Indians broadcaster. Score was the American League rookie of the year in 1955 and was an all-star in both 1955 and 1956. Others buried at the cemetery include former Cleveland Indians owner and frozen-foods magnate Vernon Stouffer; Indians co-owners the Jacobs brothers; and sportscaster Nev Chandler.

A number of people who contributed greatly to the growth and quality of life in Rocky River are buried at the cemetery, including former mayors Sion Wenban, Earl Martin, Don Umerley and William Knoble, as well as longtime school board and City Council member Dr. James Schieda, and Rocky River Public Library benefactor Emily Macbeth. Area business leaders whose final resting place is here include Bonne Bell cosmetics chairman Jess Bell, ceramics legend R. Guy Cowan, retailer Harry Colahan, former Rocky River Chamber of Commerce President Byron Spooner Sr., and restaurant owner Otto Fuchs.

Among the many other public figures buried at the cemetery (and certainly not a complete list) are hockey star James Hendy; nationally respected radio personality Joe Finan; *Cleveland Press* editor Louis Seltzer; teachers Frank Cucciarre, Vince Dooley, David Zaylor, and Rex Zirbes; cartoonist Art Sansom, Jr. who drew "The Born Loser" strip; attorney John Rea and wife Ruth; businessman Webber Collart and his wife Shirley; radiologist Keith Irish who resided on Parkside Drive; Lakewood Mayor Frank Celeste; and renowned band leader Sammy Kaye.

The Promising Future

The same qualities of vision and determination that made Rocky River a quintessential suburb and sustained its quality of life are still at work today. The characteristics that made Rocky River special – from the fine schools to the elite city services – remain in place, overseen by new generations of dedicated leaders and citizens. Further, locals never tire of the City's enduring advantages – they love living near a great lake, alongside a river and metropolitan park system, as well as the convenience involved in getting to downtown Cleveland and the airport.

Those who grow up in Rocky River, lived elsewhere for a time, and later returned – are among the passionate residents. City Council President David Furry is a prime example. So is Councilman Thomas Hunt, who lived in Bay Village for several years, but returned to Rocky River with his wife when they started a family. Businessman Randy Bierman was a RRHS graduate, left for a period of time, and then raised his family with his late wife in Rocky River. Historian Peter J. Rea lived in the Philippines for a time but has returned and is an enthusiastic booster of the City. Rocky River Municipal Court Judge Karen Kelly Kraus and many dozens of others agree the City is a great place to live and to raise children.

There is not even a hint of stagnation:

- Roadway improvements are underway through the City. In 2025, the city received a $132,000 grant from the Federal Highway Administration to study making roadways safer.
- The Senior Center, which enriches the lives of many residents, is being expanded. Improved landscaping will be visible from a new walking trail alongside the Center.
- Demolition of the outdated fire station and construction of a new two-story fire station are being planned at a cost of $13.5 million.
- A new trail for pedestrians and bicyclists will soon stretch from Webb Road in Lakewood to Linda Street in Rocky River.
- The sanitary sewer system is being upgraded.
- A $1.43 million planned project will restore Spencer Creek, addressing erosion, enhancing stormwater management, removing invasive plants, and other goals.
- The City added a tots lot playground for very young children on Bates Road 20 years ago.
  Now, under the leadership of Harlan Radford and civic groups such as the Rotary Club, Elle's Enchanted Forest playground for everyone including children with

disabilities, parents and grandparents behind City Hall is another welcome addition. Radford also pulled local leaders together to create the Safety Town program which teaches pre-schoolers vital concepts such as their home address, their parents' phone numbers, and the meaning of street signs.

- At Rocky River Park, catch basin work was completed in 2025 to prevent erosion. Meanwhile, at Bradstreet's Landing, an upcoming project will improve stormwater management, floodplain restoration, park seating, and parking lot expansion.

Meanwhile, forward-thinking redevelopment will continue to give the City a refreshed look. The luxurious new townhomes and condominiums on Lake Road, west of Breezevale Cove, are a recent example, offering upscale residences and wonderful lake views. Meanwhile, at 20325 Center Ridge Road, planners are getting ready to convert a 1969 office building into an eight-story residential tower with 103 luxury apartments.

On the education front, the community is committed to innovation and excellence. The dedicated current School Board President, Kelly Frindt, explains, "Rocky River is a special place where everyone involved with our schools plays a huge role. This is something special that doesn't happen everywhere. Our students, families, staff and community all have the same goal, which is to put our kids first and keep our tradition of excellence year after year." Kelly continues, "The School Board wants to continue to partner with everyone to keep our tradition of excellence while continuing to grow and do better. The board's goal is to do everything we can to help our students succeed and set them up for success after they leave RRHS while being good stewards of our tax dollars so everyone can continue to support our schools." Like many parents of current students, Frindt herself is a RRHS graduate.

With this track record of achievement and more improvements in the planning and implementation stages, all signs point toward a continued bright future in Rocky River. Years from now, when another author lovingly writes the sequel to this book, there will be much to share and celebrate.

About the Author

Author Doug Kurkul called Rocky River his home for 16 years and has continued to visit regularly in the years since. In *Rocky River, Ohio: The Remarkable Story of a Quintessential American Suburb,* Kurkul explains how this lakefront community just eight miles from downtown Cleveland – through vision, perseverance, unity and good fortune – has cultivated a national reputation for excellence in education, public safety, recreation, and quality of life. As in his previous books, Kurkul's narrative brings the story to life, explaining how everyone from a disgraced British military officer to an Ohio Governor to Amelia Earhart to Arnold Palmer to George Steinbrenner to Vernon Stouffer to an inventor of Mister Coffee have played roles in Rocky River's fascinating history.

Kurkul is a longtime industry association CEO based in the Chicago suburbs. His previous books include *It's a Beautiful Day for Baseball: The National Pastime in the 1960s* which has been on Amazon's top 25 Baseball History Book list continuously since May 2024, and *Portrait of a Franchise: An Intimate Look at Cleveland Indians Baseball During the Rockin' Sixties*. Kurkul also was editor of the award-winning book, *Manufacturing in America: A Legacy of Excellence.*

Figure 69 - This postcard, mailed in 1959, shows four Rocky River scenes. (author's collection)

Appendix A: When Selected Rocky River Residential Streets Were First Developed

Rocky River offers a broad array of housing options, from century homes to recent construction; single-family homes, townhomes, condominiums, and apartments. The information below identifies the period that many of the city's residential streets were initially developed.

Aberdeen Road: Early to mid 1930s.

Allen Court: 1900 to 1918.

Arbor Cliff Lane: 1999 to 2003.

Archwood Drive: Late 1960s.

Argyle Oval: Mid 1920s.

Arundel Road: Early to mid 1920s.

Ashley Court: Mid to late 1980s.

Astor Place: Early 2000s.

Avalon Drive: Mid 1920s to early 1940s.

Baldwin Lane: Early 1980s.

Bates Road: Mid 1940s.

Battersea Boulevard: Mid 1920s, adjacent to land that had been used as an early golf course.

Beach Cliff Boulevard: 1920s to 1950s.

Figure 70 - Runners race down Beach Cliff Blvd. (author's collection)

Beachwood Road: Late 1920s to late 1930s.

Beaconsfield Boulevard: Late 1930s to early 1950s.

Beverly Hills Drive: 1973 to 1974.

Blossom Drive: Mid 1950s.

Bonnie Bank Boulevard: 1930 through 1950.

Breezevale Cove: 22660 Breezevale overlooking Lake Erie was built as a cottage in 1913 and later expanded. Other homes built in 1940s. Homeowners on the west side of the street sold their homes to Brickhaus Partners by 2020 to facilitate construction of the $30 million 700 Lake project featuring eight townhomes and 25 condominiums.

Bristol Lane: In the 2000s.

Buckingham Road: Early to mid 1920s.

Carmen Drive: Mid 1950s to early 1960s.

Carolyn Avenue: 1920s to 1960s.

Chatham Place: Late 1960s to mid 1970s.

Chrisfield Drive: Mid to late 1960s.

Colahan Drive: Late 1950s.

Appendix A: When Selected Rocky River Residential Streets Were First Developed

Collver Road: Mid 1920s.

Cornwall Road: Mid 1920s.

Cottonwood Drive: 1950s.

Country Club Drive: Mid 1950s.

Dale Avenue: Mid to late 1950s.

Delbank Drive: 1950s.

East Surrey Court: Early 1960s, developed by the John Marquard Sons Company on land formerly owned by dahlia farmer John Wind.

Endsley Avenue: Late 1920s to early 1940s.

Erie Road: Starting in the late 1920s.

Eriewood Drive: Mid 1950s.

Falmouth Drive: Late 1930s.

Forestview Avenue: Mid 1950s.

Gasser Boulevard: 1930s and 1940s.

Gate House Lane: Late 1980s to 1990s.

Gibson Drive: Late 1950s, named for a former Rocky River mayor.

Goldengate Avenue: Homes built over a wide period from 1920 to 1960.

Goldwood Drive: Late 1960s.

Grandview Drive: 2008.

Hampton Road: Early 1940s to early 1950s.

Harwich Court: 1973 to 1974.

Hidden Valley Drive: Late 1970s to early 1980s.

Homeland Drive: Mostly early 1950s.

Ingersoll Drive: This is a private road along the former streetcar right-of-way with mostly commercial properties.

Jameston Drive: Early to mid 1950s.

Kensington Oval: Mid 1920s.

Kenwood Avenue: 1930s.

Kingsbury Drive: Late 1960s.

Lake Road: Mostly 1930s to 1950s. Newer condominiums and townhomes in the 2020s.

Lakeview Avenue: Late 1920s.

Laramie Drive: 1959 to 1962. The street was named after a television show titled, "Fort Laramie." It has been home to prominent Rocky Riverites including Sunny and Marlys Christensen.

Laurel Avenue: Mostly 1930s. The street was part of the Schlather estate and was named after the laurel tree.

Linda Street: What was primarily a residential street in the 1960s has evolved through redevelopment into a largely commercial corridor as part of the expanded downtown Rocky River. One of the structures (539 Linda St.) dates to 1884.

Macbeth Drive: Mostly 1940s and 1950s. This street was part of the Macbeth estate and was developed by Donald Macbeth after his father, Thomas, passed away.

Magnolia Drive: Mid 1960s.

Malvern Avenue: 1928 to 1932.

Maplewood Avenue: Mid 1920s to mid 1940s.

Marlys Drive: Early 1970s, named for Marlys Christensen, who died in 2014 at age 97.

Mitchell Avenue: 1915 to 1918. Originally a dirt road, Mitchell is one of the oldest streets in the city. It was two-sided before highway construction eliminated houses on the south side.

Morley Avenue: Formerly known as Morley Court, homes were initiated between 1910 and 1920, with some built as late as 1939.

Morewood Parkway: Late 1920s to early 1950s.

Nelson Park Drive: Mostly 1950s, though records show one home dating to 1918.

Northview Road: 1910 to 1950.

Appendix A: When Selected Rocky River Residential Streets Were First Developed

Oak Road: Mid-to-late 1920s.

Orchard Grove Avenue: Early 1950s.

Orchard Park Drive: Mid 1950s.

Palmer Drive: 1973.

Parklane Drive: Mid to late 1950s.

Parklawn Drive: 1920s.

Parkview Avenue: 1940s.

Parsons Court: 1890s.

Pond Drive: Early 1990s.

Purnell Avenue: 1930s.

River Oaks Drive: Mostly 1960s, some more recent.

River Parke: 2001 to 2003.

River Place: 2005.

Rockland Avenue: Late 1920s to mid 1930s.

Rockcliff Drive: 1925 to 1950.

Roslyn Drive: Early 1920s to mid 1930s.

Shoreland Avenue: 1920s and beyond. This is the street on which musician "Swingin' Sammy" Kaye resided.

Smith Court: This street has evolved from residential to mostly commercial. At least one of the dwellings (1228 Smith Court) dates to 1900 per government records.

Snowflower Drive: Late 1960s.

Southbend Drive: Late 1950s.

South Hampton Parkway: 1987.

South Kensington Road: Early 1940s.

Stratford Avenue: 1930s. Stratford now dead ends at Morewood Parkway, but at one time headed further east to Smith Court.

Story Road: Late 1940s to mid 1950s.

Struhar Drive: Mid 1950s.

Telbir Avenue: Mid 1920s. Old time Rocky River residents explain that this street was named after a family whose name was Riblet, spelled backward.

Thomson Circle: Mid 1960s. Named for one of the families that owned greenhouses in Rocky River.

Vine Court: Mid 1970s.

Walnut Lane: Mid 1970s.

Warwick Lane: Late 1990s.

Westfield Lane: Mid to late 1980s.

Westhampton Drive: 1998 to 2003.

Westmoor Road: Early to mid 1950s.

Westover Avenue: 1950s.

Westway Drive: 1910 and later.

West Wagar Circle: 1959.

Whittlesay Lane: 1950s.

Wildflower Drive: Mid to late 1950s.

Wooster Road: One of the first streets developed, homes range from the 19th to the 21st Century.

Wynwood Drive: Mid 1950s.

Appendix B: Rocky River Chamber of Commerce Members (as of August 2025)

18 Lab Golf. 9Round Fitness. 911 Driving School. Adapative Investments. A&A Management. Avon Oaks Country Club. Acroment Technologies. ASAP Fitness. Any Lab Test Now. A&A Capital Management. American Chemical Products. AZ Management. Adobe Acrobat. Art Marina Consulting. Airko. AFLAC. All County NEO Lake Coast Property Management. Aligned Health Center. American Safe & Vault. ADV Home Improvements. American Brass. Action Coach. Argo Wealth Management. Around the Corner. ABC Trophy & Engraving. Aria Financial Group. Andrako Insurance Consultants. Buffalo Wild Wings. Big Bear Consulting. BIBIBOP Asian Grill. By Katie K. Bill D Design Group. Battle & Polly. Busch Funeral & Crematory Services. BrB Me Time; Blue Cranium. Burkey Excavating. Brightscape Enterprises. Brighton Chase Apartments. BVS Film Productions. Burntwood Tavern. Beardens. Baird – The BCJC Group. Beck Center for the Arts. Berkshire Hathaway Realty. Brad Smith Roofing. Bucci's Italian Restaurant. Bridge Rehab & Performance. Bigmouth Donut. Charles Scott Salons. Clean Solutions. Citywide Painting. Casey's Irish Imports. City of Rocky River Police. Coin Shop Cleveland. Clerk of Court Rocky River. CKE Insurance. CN Baker Enterprises. Cleveland Ketchup. Crumbl Fairview Park. Chicago Title. Conncctcd Psychology. Colors + Counseling. City of Rocky River Director of Planning. Corrigan Craciun Funeral Home. CDog Lawn & Landscape. Coldwell Banker Commercial Real Estate. Chick-fil-A. CMIT Solutions. Cleveland Magazine. Concierge Medicine of Westlake. Caring Transitions. Cleveland CPAs. Cox Business. Clark Admin Services. Cleveland Elder Law. Civista Bank. Corrigan Krause. Danny Boy's Pizza. Dairy Queen. Ducy Design. Dante Lucci Salon. Dresch Law. Dale Corrigan Training. Dennis Allen. Delicious Product. Dollar Bank. Distinctive Metal Roofing. Devries, Trifiletti & Loy. Damien Campbell Productions. Dan Malcolm Home Inspector. Design Mojo. DiaNetrics. David M. Lamb Co. Declutter with Devon. Erie Bank. Eyring Movers. E&H Ace Hardware. Equity Trust. Elevate Foot & Ankle. Effective Leadership Academy. Erieview Title. ERA Real Solutions. Ellie Mental Health. Edgewater Surf. EdgeLoc Interiors. Everabor Company. First Federal of Lakewood. Farah, Roberts & Ganor. Ford's Clothier. Flawless Fade. Floor Coverings International. FITWORKS. Foote Printing. Flagstar Bank Home Lending. Flood Family Ice. Fully Promoted Cleveland. Ferris Steakhouse & Tavern. Gray CPA.

Gunselman's Tavern. Gather Food & Drink. GRA Group. Granite Works Stone Design. Good Soil Lutheran Ministries. Guaranteed Rate. Gormley's Pub. Ground Works Land Design. Great Lakes CPAs. General Bar. GMP. GLAS Funds. Howard Hanna – Liz Manning. Howlers Design. Healing Pathways Cleveland. Hometown Threads. Honey Baked Ham. Howard Hanna – Dan Weist. Home Health Accessibility. Henton & Associates. Huffman, Hunt & Klym. HFS Wealth Advisors. Heidi's House & Pet Sitting. Huntington National Bank. Hyatt Place Crocker Park. Happy Healthy Cells. Handel's Ice Cream. Hotworx Rocky River. Howard Hanna – SALEmaker Team. Howard Hanna – Marc & Sue Hustek. It All Adds Up. Integrated Restoration. Integrated Network Concepts. Insurance Consultants Group. John Crull LLC. Jennansis Associates. Joyce Buick GMC. Judge Donna Congeni Fitzsimmons. JPotter Health. JL Smith Holistic Wealth Management. JadeWaves. JJ's Pizza. J. McLaughlin. Jersey Mike's Subs. Jean Rounds. Joe's Deli & Restaurant. JDS Properties. Kimberly K. Yoder LPA. Kemper Cognitive Wellness. Kitchen Tune-Up Cleveland West. Kloud 9 IT. Kelly Hunt Travel. Kisling, Nestiko & Redick. King Wah Restaurant. Kennedy Property Investments II. Kathy Berkshire. Katherine Harper, Editor. Kelly Maclean Achievement Center. Lutheran West High School. Lakewood Exterminating. Lovely Paperie & Gifts. Liminal LLC. LSC Service Corp. LPL Financial. Lash Lounge. Lipson O'Shea Legal Group. Lake Erie Crushers. Lake Road Market. Lauchacher & Co. Laskey Costello. Lakewood Truck Park. Lazzaro Luka Law Offices. Linden House. Lakewood/Rocky River Sunrise Rotary. Lux Home Remodeling. Lake Digital. Monarch Endeavors. MVP Snow n' Lawn. Mary Blank. Mancuso Homes. MG Sports Massage. Mimi Magazine. McManamon & Co. Musca Benefits. Memorial Hall at the Don Umerley Civic Center. MCM Company. MaxStrength Fitness. McGorray-Hanna Funeral Homes. Mayor, City of Rocky River. Marian C. Brumbaugh, Atty. Michael P. O'Donnell. Molinari Travel. Mangia Bella. Minuteman Press. McGregor Foundation. Magnificat High School. McDonald's – Rocky River. Maison Maison. Marlen Jewelers. Mellino Law Firm. Mitchell Brothers Ice Cream. Market. Northwestern Mutual. Navigate Risk Advisors. Northcoast Healthcare. NE1 Lighting. Northview Family Dental. Neitzel, Luke & Salopek. Northern Title Agency. Nahoda Design. Numerequip. Neubert Painting. Normandy Senior Living. NP Weiss Law. Ohio Employee Ownership Center. Old River Tap & Social. Organize by Dreams. Old School Pizza & Wings. Ohio Marine Trades Association. OCI. One World Shop. Oaks Rehabilitation & Relaxation. Ohio Junk Force. ohiobiz LLC. Organic Spa Media. Ohio Educational Credit Union. Old Carolina Barbecue. O'Neill Healthcare. O'Dell Construction. Prayers from Maria Foundation. Puritas Nursery & Garden Center. Paychex. Patton Printing. Paper Trails. Paws & Effect Pet Grooming. Power Professional Services. Park West Building. Peak and Valley Roofing. PressureWays Power Cleaning. Pearle Vision. Porterfi. PJ's Day Spa. Pure Enchantment. Patrick O'Connor. Pelaia Media Group. Pastor Emeritus Jon Fancher. Presidential Luxury Apartments. Radiant Bride. Roundstone Management. Restorative Fitness. Rocky River Brewing. Ruffing Montessori School. Rocky River Presbyterian Church. Raj

Appendix B: Rocky River Chamber of Commerce Members (as of August 2025)

Plastic Surgery. Reilly's Irish Bakery. Rocky River Municipal Court. RW Magic. Rustbelt Reclamation. Rocky River Chiropratic. Rocky River Parks & Recreation Foundation. Race Fuel. Rocky River City Council – Christina Morris. Rocky River City Council – Jean Gallagher. Rad Air of Westlake. Rocky River Assisted Living & Memory Care. Rocky River Public Library. River City Wood Products. Rauser & Associates Legal Clinic. Raising Cane's. River Dental Arts. Rocky River Municipal Court – Chief Deputy Clerk. Revenant Global. Ruoff Mortgage. Rene Michael Salon. River Endodontics. Rockway Mortgage. River Trading Co. Rocky River Director of Finance. Rocky River School District. Rocky River Women's Club. Rocky River United Methodist Church. Rocky River Historical Society. Rocky River Recreation Center. Russell Commercial Advisory. Right at Home. Sgt. Clean Car Wash. Sakana Sushi Bar & Lounge. Sleep Outfitters. Salmon Daves. Schenider Smeltz Spieth Bell LLP. Seniority Benefit Group. SeibertKeck Insurance Partners. Self Care Hair. SBA Lenders. State Farm – Robbie Anderson. SpeedPro Imaging. StretchLab Rocky River. Spooner Risk Control. School of Rock. Sangfroid Strategy. Seeley, Savidge, Ebert & Gourash. Soar Aviation Law. Safe Harbor Coaching. Suzanne Edwards – Howard Hanna. Sacred Hour Spas. SJS Investment Services. Stewart Title. Sweet Designs Chocolates. Seeley Test Pros. Southwest Companies. Smiles by White. Shape Cleveland. Sandella Sova Search Partners. The Welsh Home. The Olive Scene. The Clifton Club. The SkinLab. The Cleveland Yachting Club. TopGolf Cleveland. Tri-C Westshore Campus. Taza. T3 Performance. The Westside Buzz. The Money Store. Third Federal Savings. Tomorrows a Salon. The Tailored Closet. The Arcus Group. Timan Custom Window Treatments. The Exercise Coach. The Grooming Loft by Sofie. The Hall at St. James. The Proficient Office. Total Restore. Urban Chiropractic. Vital Hydration & Wellness. Village Project. Ver-a-Fast. Woodhouse Day Spa. Westwood Town Center. The Woods. Waterbrook Accounting. Westlake Condominium Association. Westsiders. Watts Law. Window Genie. Wine & Whiskey. Welcome House. Waldheger Coyne. Westlake Express Cab. Wine Bar Rocky River/Tommy's Place. Wild Flour Bakery. With a Twist. Wise Coatings. Western & Southern. White Sea Global. WestLIFE Newspaper. World Group. Westwood Country Club. Westgate Mall. Your Bridge Wealth Management. Zeis-McGreevey Funeral Home. Zippy Taxes. Z Dentist.

Appendix C: List of Greenhouses and Truck Gardens in 1927

(thank you to Gay Christensen Dean)

1. Schneider greenhouse and truck farm. 2. Wm. J. Kramer. 3. C. Dean estate. 4. Wm. Case. 5. Ohio Greenhouse – Judy. 6. Barco (not on 1927 map but on 1956 map). 7. Jenkins Florist – Hillcrest. 8. J. Schnid – Ingersoll Drive. 9. L&M Anderson (later owned by Dorothy Horton Kaiser). 10. WW and Mable Lovell. 11. Henry and Julia Lovell. 12. Emma Dean. 13. Ethel Loughlin. 14. A&N McFerron. 15. George Christensen. 16. JM Gasser. 17. HL Christensen. 18. A. Christensen. 19. John Hogg (Hoag). 20. Rocky River Greenhouse. 21. Julius Zeager. 22. Hans Wind. 23. No name – half in River half in Fairview. 24. Peter Peterson. 25. Carl Christensen. 26. Thomson Gardening. 27. Goldwood Greenhouse/George A. Christensen. 28. James Ward. 29. Harry Asplin. 30. Unidentified. 31. Mary Jane Pease/Mary Grigsby. 32. Stepler Truck Farm. 33. Arthur Hoag. 34. Hoag-Petersen Truck Farm.

Bibliography

Along Ohio's Historic Route 20 by Michael Till.

A History of the Normandy Apartments, by Carolyn and John Rowland, May 16, 2012.

America's Wartime Progress, by George Weiss, the New York Marine News Company, 1920.

American Legion, exchange of emails, May 2025.

Bay Village Historical Society.

Bowling Green State University Library, Historical Collections of the Great Lakes. Retrieved June 11, 2020.

Case Western Reserve Encyclopedia of Cleveland History.

Christensen Dean, Gay, phone interview, July 2025. The daughter of Sunny and Marlys Christensen, she is one of the foremost authorities on Rocky River history and was especially helpful in gathering information for this book.

Clevelandhistorical.org.

Cleveland Chamber of Commerce, Annual Report No. 69, 1917.

Early History of Cleveland, Ohio: Including Papers and Other Matters, by Col. Charles Whittlesey.

History of Cuyahoga County in Three Parts, by Crisfield Johnson.

Incidents & Episodes: Tales of Rocky River and Rockport Township, Ohio, George A. "Sunny" Christensen, edited by Gay A. Christensen-Dean.

Frindt, Kelly, School Board President, exchange of email messages, August 2025.

Furry, David, exchanges of emails, spring and summer, 2025.

Lakewood, by Thea Gallo Becker, Arcadia, an imprint of Tempus Publishing.

Lakewood Historical Society.

Lakewood Observer.

Library of Congress, exchange of email messages, June 2025.

Osgood, Bill, phone call and exchange of emails about The Original Candyland, May-June, 2025. Bill could not have been more helpful in sharing historical perspectives.

Radford, Harlan, phone call, July 30, 2025, and exchange of emails. Mr. Radford is a retired high school and junior high school teacher and a community leader. His knowledge of history and willingness to draw from his impressive collection of postcards helped to bring this narrative to life.

Rea, Peter J. "Rocky River, Ohio, Poetic Tour" video, YouTube, 2019.

Rocky River, by Carol Lestock, Arcadia Publishing, an imprint of Tempus Publishing, 2002.

Rocky River Yesterday, Rocky River Historical Society, Bookmasters, 2012. Phil Ardussi and other volunteers lovingly devoted many hours to make this book possible.

Rowland, Carolyn and John, "*A History of the Normandy Apartments."*

The Cleveland Memory Project, Cleveland State University, csuohio.edu.

The Plain Dealer and Cleveland.com.

The Rise and Fall of the Cleveland Greenhouse Industry, by Dennis Wagner, 2013. Retrieved June 16, 2020.

The *Sun Herald.*

Varsitytutors.com

Vignettes of Clifton Park I, by Blythe Gehring, Penton Publishing, 1970.

WestLIFE newspaper and WestLIFEnews.com. The author recommends this weekly to anyone wishing to stay abreast of all that is happening in the western suburbs.

Front Cover Photos: All are author's collection.

www.ingramcontent.com/pod-product-compliance
Lightning Source LLC
Chambersburg PA
CBHW041528070526
44586CB00002B/11